listen

(how to)

Dr Christian Heim

ISBN: 978-1-925681-25-3
Published by Vivid Publishing
A division of Fontaine Publishing Group
P.O. Box 948, Fremantle
Western Australia 6959
www.vividpublishing.com.au

Cataloguing-in-Publication data is available from the National Library of Australia

Disclaimer

The clinical practice of psychiatry is highly individualized; no inference should be made that any treatment which was effective for a person presented in this book will be effective for anyone else. Listening is not a panacea for depression, anxiety or even relationship difficulties. Do not stop any treatment, medication or otherwise, because of this book. This book gives very general ideas and pointers; it is no substitute for work with a therapist. Things discussed in this book may contradict your values or beliefs. It may bring up conflict for yourself or in your relationship. If you have any questions about your unique situation, please consult a qualified health practitioner.

Contents

Introduction

Welcome to listening in the twenty-first century. Where the heavy use of screen technology, cell phones, and voice mail can have negative impacts on who we choose to listen to, what we filter out, and how we interact.[1] Where 46% of people say they would rather leave their job than deal with conflict because managers can't hold "meaningful conversations" with them.[2] Where immediately after listening to someone speak, we remember … well … not as much as we could.

Not good.

I have been giving talks on listening for many years, because it is important in business, mental health and, most importantly, in all relationships. My journey in learning the skill of listening began thirty years ago. That's when I first realized that I was not a good listener.

You see, I got married.

Every long-term relationship is a wonderful challenge, a frustrating bliss, an exciting and perilous journey. Being in a long-term relationship makes you aware of your strengths and weaknesses. I highly recommend it.

Two years into our marriage, my love-partner became a telephone crisis counsellor. As part of the training, she learnt the skill of listening. *Christian, this course taught me how to listen, and now I know why you're not a good listener! You're too full of your own ideas. You want to solve problems. You don't listen!*

Sound familiar? So what was I to do?

This was long before I even thought of becoming a doctor, let alone a psychiatrist. To honour my love-partner and to learn a skill – a skill that would later serve me well in my profession – I took the course and I too became a telephone crisis counsellor.

I learnt how to listen.

My loving partner was happier. I was happier.

You too can learn the skill of listening. It will serve you well as a professional listener, a listener for people, or to improve your long-term relationship. The skill is the same. It's what this book is about.

As a psychiatrist, I have heard thousands of people's life stories. I have listened deeply to them. When I was a junior doctor working in a busy hospital I had little time to listen to life stories. I listened for the information I needed to make the right decision for people's health needs at that time. This was very important.

Now, specializing in psychotherapy, I listen much more. Listening is very important. In depth. Sometimes, the listening itself is the treatment. Most often, however, it is only part of a very complex treatment regime.

Listening is always important.

For professionals, listening is the skill which helps build immediate rapport, long-term trust and ensures engagement in a professional relationship. In a personal long-term relationship, it also helps build trust, and it ensures ongoing engagement. It is an act of unconditional positive regard and acceptance.

Listening is a way of saying *I love you*, or *I care*.

You don't have to be in a relationship to be a good listener. You don't have to be a good listener to be in a good relationship, but it damn well helps! It also helps to get on with friends, work colleagues and to help clinch business deals.

This book is about learning, practicing and using the skill of listening. It is about using that skill to enrich your relationships: friends, family, work colleagues, and your love-partner. It is about increased quality of life.

Chapter One introduces the first step in developing listening EARS: an overview of the skill. If you read nothing else, read this short chapter and practice it. It contains all you need to know to become a really decent listener. Knowing the listening EARS roadmap will help greatly in being effective at work, and in maintaining a healthy, loving long-term relationship. (I hate to see them get unhealthy.) But it takes practice.

Chapter Two will let you know how to practice the skill of listening to become <u>very</u> good at it; step-by-step and in a fun way.

Chapter Three applies the skill to the important and sometimes complex case of listening to your love-partner. There's science to all of this and that's what Chapter Four is all about. It discusses the science of listening and what areas in the brain are active when you listen well.

The last chapter discusses the art of listening more deeply: with your mind for information and with your heart for feelings. Both are important. Listening for information is particularly important for work, and listening for feelings is particularly important in relationships. This chapter also discusses what it means to listen to someone with your whole being: to make a real connection from one human being to another. It is for people going for the black-belt in listening: flooring others with their listening skills, taking them down with empathy and compassion, and over-whelming the opposition with humility and genuine positive regard. This is not easy to do.

The book is more touchy-feely than cut and dry. It also employs a bit of a workbook-like approach. Practice makes perfect. The skill of listening needs to be practiced over and over; it can't remain a mere theory or some knowledge head-trip. It's practical. It's also enjoyable and rewarding. Parts of the book may come across as a little didactic; it gets a bit "teachy" at times. I hope you can cope with this. If not, bad luck.

Included are a few stories of people I have worked with, par-ticularly in couple's therapy. Every story is genuine in emotional content but, in order to maintain confidentiality, names and details are changed. It is a privilege to work with people, and I thank anyone I have worked with for their trust.

It is worth learning and practicing the skill of listening. It is a way of saying *I respect you* to people at work, *I accept you* to friends and family members, *thanks for sharing* to another human being, and *I love you* to that special someone who is your love-partner.

Enjoy.

CHAPTER ONE

Listening EARS

Stupid. Of course you need ears to listen! Yet having ears is not all it takes. Hearing is not listening. Hearing is kind of automatic but we need to learn to listen. In this chapter, we'll look at what listening is and isn't, and I introduce you to the listening EARS roadmap. We'll look at all the listening basics you need to know. I apply these basics to a listening scenario involving a real-life couple.

In couple's therapy, I hear the complaints:

> *She never listens!*
> *He never shuts up!*
> *He doesn't do what I tell him to.*
> *She talks a lot so I just zone out.*

Few people <u>really</u> listen.

Listening is an active, conscious and concentrated process; it is being there for somebody while they share something of themselves. Listening is a gift that can leave a person with the feeling of "having been heard," having someone "drink in" and understand what they are experiencing. Listening is "walking beside" someone for a while and getting to know what it is to "walk in their shoes." So, a take home message (THM).

THM: Listening is a gift we give to someone else.

The listening world is saturated by some well-trodden metaphors: "being there" for someone, "walking in their shoes" for a while, "sharing their journey," "giving them space" and letting them "feel heard." Try not to be put off by these clichés. (I was, at first). They may be a little "touchy-feely" and vague, but they are useful, and I will use them (*sorry*) but not too much (*phew*).

The three stages of listening

I talk of listening in three stages: hearing, listening and active listening.

<u>Hearing</u> is done with the ears: the outer ears (which stick out a bit), little hairs inside the ears (ones you can't comb), some nerves, and the brain. It is the physical sensation and the initial registration of sounds. If you are not deaf, you can hear things all your wakeful hours without listening to them.

<u>Listening</u> involves giving some attention to what you hear. When you focus your attention on a sound, you can name it, understand its source, and have initial thoughts and feelings about the sound. Some people like to call this "passive listening."

<u>Active listening</u> – what this book is all about – is much more complex. Some people like to call it "attentive listening" or

"conscious listening." Active listening means that you are deeply focussed on the listening process; you are more "present" and "attentive." (There I go with more clichés). In normal language, that means you give it even more attention and focus. Your feelings are moved by what you are listening to, and your thoughts are making connections between what you are listening to and what you have experienced in your life. It is "listening with your whole being" and "being engaged." It is listening with concentration.

We will revisit the important distinctions between hearing, listening, and active listening in Chapter Two. For now, the take home message (THM) I want you to remember is that hearing, listening, and active listening are different.

THM: Hearing, listening, and active listening involve increasing amounts of focus, attention and concentration.

In this book, I'll always assume that you are listening to one person: "one-on-one." Occasionally, like when you are listening to your son and his partner, you may listen "one-on-two." In the book, however, I will always refer to one-on-one listening where you, "the listener," are listening to "the talker." When I know you have the hang of things, I will often use the word listening when I mean active listening.

Listening is easy

Most people are better listeners than they think they are; they do it every day. Children listen to their teachers and parents: they "drink in" what was said and then do as they are told (mostly). At work, listening is often part of finding a solution to a problem. If you want to keep your job, you usually listen to your boss. In a sense, at work you are paid to listen. People in sales listen to managers to sell more of a product; soldiers listen to officers to be effective; doctors listen to people they treat; and professional players listen to their coaches to help win games.

People are paid to listen, get information, and put it into practice for the right outcome.

Relationship listening is different. You don't get paid for it. Yet, you have to put in the effort, and the benefit is for the person you are listening to, not you. Relationship listening is often aimed at sharing emotions[3] rather than finding a solution. The outcome may be a deepening of the relationship or the other person getting some feelings off their chest.

THM: Relationship listening is often for sharing emotions, not for solving problems.

This is a tough one. We all tend to think someone is talking to us to find a solution to their problem. We <u>want</u> to give a solution. We <u>hate</u> to see them get it wrong. But it makes <u>us</u> feel better to fix things. Remember that listening is for them, not for us.

Here's the thing though, often people talk to us "as a sounding board" to help fix a problem, but the <u>real</u> contribution you make is letting them share their feelings. You "journey" with them in their problem, so they are not alone. That builds trust and friendship. (You may still help them with their problem, but this is problem-solving not active listening.)

So, two things make relationship listening different: you don't get paid for it, and it is not aimed at finding a solution. Knowing this will already let you know what to work on to be a better listener: being more selfless, and not trying to solve problems.

THM: To listen well in relationships, keep interested in <u>them</u>, and try not to problem-solve.

You need to find a way to keep listening and interested even when you don't get paid. And that's usually everywhere except at work. Here's an example.

If you're in sales or business you will remember someone's name if that name means money, opportunity or power to you. (It's rare to forget your boss's name.) But if you're on holidays and you're introduced to someone new, you may struggle to remember their name the next day. Why? Because they don't mean money or power to you and you're on holidays.

THM: Learning to listen well is easy, as long as you have an incentive to do it.

The big incentive you have to listen well is getting on well with people: being liked, appreciated, and sharing trust and friendship. This leads to a better quality of life for you and other people. It's the same with your love-partner: the aim is to have a good relationship. That will mean less arguments, more peace, more understanding, more hugs and kisses, and better lives for both of you.

Active listening is not ...

From the start, we have to get a few things straight. Active listening is not doing what someone tells you to do, it's not the silent bit of the conversation where you don't get to talk, and it's not smiling politely while you complain to yourself about what a bore this person is. Let's go over some of this in more detail.

Active listening is not doing what someone tells you to

Let's face it. For some people, *they don't listen to me* is really code for *they don't do what I tell them to!*

Doing what someone else tells you to is not listening. It is obedience. It is separate from listening. You may want your kids to listen and do as they are told, but this is not what adult interactions are all about. You can listen well and still not do what someone else wants you to. Really? Yes. The two are connected, but for the purposes of this book, they're not. Doing as you are told may be good at work if you want to keep your job, but it can become subservience in relationships.

THM: Listening and doing what you are told are separate.

Many people use talking as a form of controlling other people. They expect that someone who listens to them will do what they say. You can't control other people. You can't make anyone do what you want them to even if you are a parent, boss, a dictator or a terrorist. To comply with your wishes, a person must either agree with you or be sacrificial towards you out of love, duty, fear of death, or a moderate-to-large sum of money.

THM: You can't control other people.

This is a very difficult lesson for all of us. We all would like to control other people. It may be true that everybody wants to rule the world, but this just doesn't happen. Nobody even gets to control their own neighbourhood. You can't control anyone. Listening is actually the opposite of controlling another person. It is letting them be themselves and express themselves as completely as they can.

THM: Listening is the opposite of controlling.

Active listening is not a part of conversation

Listening may be a part of conversation, but the active listening we're learning about here is different. A conversation is a two-way or a three-way or a more-way street. Someone talks, you listen; you talk, they listen. That sounds fair doesn't it?

But, in a conversation, when they talk, you're not listening the way I want you to. Sure, you listen to their words, but you make judgments about what they're saying:

> *I agree, yeah that's right.*
> *I don't agree, wrong!*
> *What a jerk, when is it my turn?*
> *I wonder what's for dinner tonight?*
> *I wonder if they're single?*
> *What should I say?*
> *Hope I come across as clever.*

Then you launch in with your words and evaluate yourself:

> *That sounded good.*
> *Hope I made an impression.*
> *Maybe that's not right.*
> *I hope they still like me.*

These judgments get in the way of active listening.

Active listening is not part of a conversation. It's a one-way street. You get information from them, without giving any away. You aim to discover what they are trying to say, what they experience, think, feel, or how they've been affected. Ideally, you do this without judgment. (This is very hard to do).

In a two-way conversation, talking and listening is about 50%-50%; in a four-way conversation it's about 25% each. This happens naturally. Mostly, in a group, people get uncomfortable if one person dominates conversation, so they find ways of directing conversation away from them. They get uncomfortable if one person is talking less than others so they direct questions to that person to be inclusive. (Of course, the big talker doesn't want to include anyone, they just want to be heard.)

To get the one-way street active listening going, aim to have them talking about 80% and you about 20%.

THM: Listening is basically a one-way street. Traffic heads towards you.

Active listening is "being there"

There is only one thing you need to remember about what active listening really is. Active listening is simply being there for the other person.

That's it.

Of course, to be there for the other person as a fellow human being entails much more than your mere physical presence, it also involves your emotional and mental presence and acceptance. When it comes to mere physical presence, faithful dogs make the best listeners. They do this very, very well and are even there emotionally to some extent. They listen (and bark and whine once in a while). For this they get rewarded with pats, food and walks.

As a human, you have much more to offer with your listening, but being there is the right attitude to start with. Let's get this right before we get to the more complex stuff. Your role as a listener is to give support and care rather than to give solutions and ideas. Active listening is selfless: you give time and attention to the talker. You focus on _them_. Your thoughts and feelings have to do with _them_ not you. Yeah, this is difficult but hugely rewarding (way beyond pats and walks).

THM: In listening, it's all about them. Just be there, like a faithful canine.

OK, so now you know that active listening is a one-way street and faithfully being there to support and care for someone. And you know it is not problem-solving, not doing as you are told, not part of a conversation and definitely not controlling anyone. So, let's get into the basic technique: the listening EARS roadmap.

The Listening EARS roadmap

Active listening is a skill which can be learnt, but it takes practice. All you need is a pair of listening EARS. EARS is the acronym I use for the roadmap of good listening.

E   Establish an Environment for listening
A   Ask questions and say *A-huh* to show you're listening
R   Repeat what the talker says in their words to show you're listening
S   Summarize the Situation to finish and show you've listened

E. Establishing an Environment for listening is so important. A subway train is not a good place for listening. Find a quiet space, a spare half hour, and a warm atmosphere. This says *I care, I have time, I'll be there for you.* Establishing an Environment for listening means stopping what you are doing for a while, and making sure you won't be interrupted. If you can't do that on the spot, then say something like, *I'll be with you in ten minutes* or *can we talk after dinner?* Set up a time in the future if it's in five minutes or five days. This is also good business practice. It is the start of any good listening interaction. (Sometimes, however, a noisy subway may be the only environment you have.)

If you can, go to a place private (rather than an open-plan office cubicle). Turn off all phones and ignore incoming messages. Maybe sit down together in chairs with or without a cup of tea, coffee, wine or beer (but not all at once). Make the effort to look the person in the eye and slow down the pace of your life for a few minutes. Take time and put in effort. For them.

THM: A quiet space with uninterrupted time establishes a listening environment.

A. Ask questions. Begin with something like

> *Right, what do you want to talk about?*
> *So, you were saying?*
> *What do you need me to listen to?*
> *What's on your mind?*

Then say nothing for as long as you can. Shut up and listen. After they have spoken, follow-up with questions such as

> *And then what happened?*
> *What did you feel?*
> *Anything else you want to tell me?*
> *And …* (expectantly waiting on words)

Asking question gets the other person talking. Keep them talking. You shut up. Listen to the answers and be curious and interested. Just don't hit them with a barrage of questions – the less the better – just keep them talking. Ask questions to clarify, explain or describe events, thoughts and feelings further.

If you get an idea that may help them, keep it to yourself. Shut up. Remember, you're not problem-solving. Later you may get into problem-solving, but problem-solving is not part of listening, it's a separate thing. Listening is listening and nothing else. Listening does not solve problems, it lets people feel heard.

THM: *Listening lets people feel heard.*

Ideally, your questions will be "open-ended" rather than "closed." Closed questions, the ones we want less of, can be answered by yes or no:

> *Do you want me to listen?*
> *Are you OK?*
> *Do you need a tissue?*

Open-ended questions, the ones we want more of, need an explanation and they encourage the talker to do more talking:

> *How are you feeling at the moment?*
> *What happened after she drove away?*
> *How would you like me to respond?*
> *What do you need from me right now?*

Using open-ended question gets them talking, puts them in charge of the conversation, and doesn't make them feel interrogated.

THM: Ask open-ended questions to get them talking.

The A in EARS is also for *A-huh, Ahh,* and any other little grunts that say *I'm listening* while they talk. Ideally, aside from questions, and repeating information in their words, this is the only other thing you say. (In practice this is hard to do, but try to keep this in mind).

R. Repeat the information they gave you using their words. If they say, *and then she just drove off,* just say, *and then she just* *drove off !?*. !? means that you give the words a hint of surprise, empathy, outrage, or whatever you think is helpful. Repeating any information in exactly their words shows that you are taking in information without judging or changing it in any way. This is very powerful. Just don't be a parrot, add some of your own emotion without changing the words; or change the words a little. After repeating something, follow up with another question and with *A-huhs*.

THM: *Repeat their words to show you are listening.*

S. Summarize the Situation; but not too soon. To summarize, say something like *so, you needed me to listen to how you felt after your mother just drove off. Is that right?* If you get it wrong, that doesn't matter; the talker will gladly correct you. *No. That's not what I wanted!* You are allowed to make mistakes in listening. (I do, a lot). If you are corrected, that's OK, you'll just need to listen some more, ask more questions, say more *A-huh's*, repeat their words, and summarize the situation again later. If you get it right, the other person will let you know and that signals the end of that listening session.

THM: *Summarizing shows you have listened.*

That's it. Simple.

This is active listening: they share information and feel heard. You don't give information because that becomes a conversation or problem-solving. Listening is powerful because it shows that you care, are supportive and you are there for them; really there.

Objections!

I knew it. You have objections. You just can't see why this touchy-feely stuff is important. I hear you, I'm listening. I feel the objections burning inside you. So let's face them, right here and now.

<u>Objection #1.</u> *Why should I practice something I do every day?*

Most people hear but don't listen; at least they don't actively listen. Active listening is a skill which you can learn and practice. When I first started to use the skill, I wasn't very good at it. The more I practiced, the more natural it became. I got better. This is the same for every person and every skill: playing the piano, cooking, playing tennis, writing neatly, navigating the internet, or drawing. Listening is just another skill that needs practice. The benefits of practice are enormous.

<u>Objection #2.</u> *I'm embarrassed to do something I'm not good at.*

Welcome to the club. None of us like doing things we're not too good at. If you're doing it, and it feels uncomfortable and you think you're getting it wrong, just say to the person you are listening to *I'm trying to do what that blasted shrink said in that listening book!* You will be surprised how much someone will appreciate your efforts, particularly your love-partner. It's OK to feel bad, and it's OK to make mistakes. Also, you <u>will</u> get better, quickly.

Objection #3. *This feels artificial, it's not me.*

That's exactly how I felt when I started. Persevere. It's worth it. At first it <u>does</u> feel artificial, but your brain adapts and makes things eventually sound natural. In fact, it is really important to be yourself. It's good to be yourself. After all, someone is talking to <u>you</u>, a person who is caring enough to listen; they are not talking to a technique.

Objection #4. *How can I be myself while learning this technique?*

That's difficult. It's like when you first learn to play golf or tennis. It feels unnatural at first, then the swing feels more natural, then you end up with a swing that's all your own. It just happens. The truth is, you can't help but be yourself. It will always happen. Just let it happen. It'll be OK. It's OK to be yourself in listening; in fact, it's highly desirable.

THM: It'll be OK.

"OK" becomes another one of those clichés. In listening, everything is "OK." It is. It's OK to make mistakes, it's OK to be yourself, it's OK to feel artificial when you first start, it's OK to learn a skill. There is a fundamental reason that it's all OK in listening: it's OK for the talker to say almost anything they like. OK is part of not judging them and just being there for them. So if it is OK for them, the same goes for you. It's OK. I'll talk more about having a non-judgmental attitude in just a little while.

<u>Objection #5.</u> *Why should I learn to listen? I can get through life without it.*

Sure you can. Listening is a gift you give to someone else; particularly people you are close to. It says *I care*. Active listening is a way of sharing friendship and love. It lets people reveal themselves. It creates a bond and increases trust. You can get by without listening well, but listening well is a bonus. Your friends, partner and family will thank you for it. You'll grow to like it too.

Try this. Instead of spending a heap of money on an anniversary gift, tell your partner *my present this year is that I am going to learn how to listen well.* See if that makes a difference.

The Six Basics of Listening

In a nutshell, these are the basics for good active listening.

THM: The six basics of good active listening are …

> *1. The listening EARS roadmap*
> *2. Listening is "being there" for the other person*
> *3. Listening is not a conversation, it is a one-way street*
> *4. Listening means shelving your beliefs and judgments*
> *5. Listening is not problem-solving, and*
> *6. Listening engenders trust.*

Put these basics into practice. It never matters if you make mistakes, it's OK, just as long as you try. Trying helps make you a good listener; it builds trust. Let's look at these more closely.

1. THE LISTENING EARS ROADMAP.

If you go no further in this book except the Listening EARS roadmap, you can improve your listening immensely. It is the core of the program. What scales are to musicians, what ball-control is to footballers, the EARS roadmap is to listeners. Remember it. Stick to it. Never let it go.

> E   Establish an Environment for listening
> A   Ask questions and say *A-huh* to show you're listening
> R   Repeat what the other person says to show you're listening
> S   Summarize the Situation to finish and show you've listened

2. BE THERE.

It's all about them not you. To be there for the other person you may need to give yourself a little pep talk just before you start the listening session: *I am here to listen to them, to be there for them, to give them the opportunity to feel heard.* This principle becomes a large part of the advanced listening skills section of the last chapter.

THM: Give yourself a little pep-talk to remind yourself to just be there for them.

3. LISTENING IS A ONE-WAY STREET.

This basic principle is why listening can be difficult: it puts you in a subservient or giving role. Our natural tendency is to try to equalize with another person: *hey, my turn!* Listening is letting go of your need to feel important and "heard" while <u>they</u> talk.

Get them talking about 80% of the time. That's why asking questions, the *A-huh's*, and silences are so important. During a listening session, you may need to check yourself to make sure you aren't talking too much. If you are, just remind yourself you are there to listen, maybe apologize, then give them the space to talk, and continue listening. Leave silence in case they want to say something. Give them time.

THM: Be comfortable with silence.

4. SHELVE YOUR BELIEFS AND JUDGMENTS.

This is difficult. In a conversation, your beliefs and judgments are as important as anyone else's. But beliefs can get us into conflict and nobody likes conflict. It is unpleasant and we generally avoid it or argue it out. Even when it doesn't bring about conflict, being in judgement mode means you are not in listening mode.

In listening, you offer the opportunity for the talker to express any opinion, even if it differs from your own. You want them to feel free to do this, or else they will filter what they say, or stop speaking altogether. They do not want to feel judged or have you disagree with them. So let go of judgment comments.

> *You're out of control*
> *You're not handling this right*
> *What you should do is …*
> *Yes, but …*
> *Well that was stupid*
> *That's awful!*

They need to feel that it is OK to be themselves. Usually in a crisis, or even a mini-crisis, they do not feel this.

Strangely though, it's best not to agree with them either; and don't reassure, because that shows you are judging.

> *Well said*
> *You did really well*
> *You're right!*

Agreeing with them is better than disagreeing, but it is still judging (you are judging them to be the winner instead of the loser). The best alternatives are *A-huh* and silence.

Don't judge the person's reactions.

You shouldn't do that!
Don't say that!
You worry too much!
You're too good!

Their reactions are OK.

Don't even judge the situation.

I've never heard anything so terrible
There is a way out you know
I don't think anyone is to blame

Even reassurances are judgmental. They stop the flow of emotion by saying *stop feeling that!* They are also closely related to problem-solving.

I'm sure you'll feel better soon
It's not as bad as you think
It'll be alright

You can see that it is important to shelve your beliefs and judgments. (Did I get that point across?)

This underlines the difference between a listening session and a conversation. In a two-way conversation you can let fly with your beliefs just as much as someone else lets fly with theirs. That way you share, agree, or agree to disagree. You can reassure or dramatize. You can direct or take control for a while. A conversation is a two-way street. But active listening is not like that, it's a one-way street for the benefit of one person (see point 3 above).

You do not need to change your beliefs; just shelve them and shut up about them for a while. Let the other person be honest and be themselves. Don't get in the way of their message, their information or their feelings. Let them be. Be interested, curious, and accepting.

Even internal judgments – *I agree, yeah that's right, that person's a jerk, that's stupid, what an emotional cripple* or *wrong, wrong, wrong* – are not helpful. Just for a little while, let it be OK for them to be who they are without you feeling threatened or challenged. This is a skill.

Visualize yourself putting your beliefs in a box, closing it and putting it on a shelf in your mind. Even while you listen to someone whose beliefs may be pretty similar to your own, it is useful to do this.

Imagine your role to be like a sponge: just soak up the information and the emotions, ready to soak up more. Be a friendly, interested sponge that someone would like to talk to.

THM: Shelve your judgments and beliefs to be a listening sponge.

5. LISTENING IS NOT PROBLEM-SOLVING.

Problem-solving may follow a listening session, but the two are very different. A good listening session may lead to a good problem-solving session; but often it doesn't. In a work or professional situation, problem-solving almost always follows listening; the aim is outcomes and productivity. Problem-solving means you add information to drive forward to an outcome. But this is not listening.

Listening is helpful even if problems remain unsolved. It builds trust and connection. This may be the only tangible outcome in relationship listening, but that's what you want, right? Relationship listening, as I said before, often shares thoughts and feelings just to be understood and accepted.

THM: *Listening and problem-solving are separate.*

Often, in relationship listening, people are at cross-purposes. The talker wants to be listened to but the listener thinks the talker wants a problem solved.

> Maggie: *I just hate it when Suzie keeps taking my time up with trivial things.*
> Sam: *Then just stop talking to her.*
> Maggie: *I don't want you to solve my problem, just listen to me!!*

Later, however.

Maggie: *Sam, the suitcase is on the floor.*
Sam: *How do you feel about that, Maggie?*
Maggie: *It makes me angry!*
Sam: *That sounds tough, Maggie. Is there anything else you wanted to share with me?*
Maggie: *Yes! I want you lift the damn thing and put it on top of that cupboard!!*
Sam: *I didn't know you wanted me to solve your problem, I thought you just wanted me to listen.*

The cross-purposes can be rectified by the talker saying *I need you to just listen, not problem-solve* or by the listener asking *do you want me to help solve a problem or just listen?*

THM: Ask "do you want me to problem-solve or just listen?"

6. LISTENING ENGENDERS TRUST.

Trust is a feeling. Anyone talking to you trusts you with some part of themselves: thoughts, feelings, fears, opinions, events, insecurities, dreams, or just some interesting things. As a listener, your job is to be trustworthy. This means being gentle with the parts of themselves they are sharing: ponder their thoughts, listen to their feelings, respect their fears, opinions and insecurities, share their dreams; just for a while. To trust is to treat them with respect and to hold their information in confidence.

They trust you; be trustworthy. Don't blab. Hold information inside your sponge self. Don't repeat it to anyone. Whatever is said in that room, stays in that room. You are not allowed to take the information and do what you want with it. It is their information and, as you are only there for them, you cannot take their information with you. They trust you. Got it?

THM: Trust means keeping confidences. Always.

Applying the Six Basics

OK. So let me reproduce a little listening scenario to show you the six basics of listening in action. Hannah and Joe have been married for eighteen years. Joe often turns up late for dinners, appointments, transport and keeps her waiting. Hannah gets embarrassed and angry about this. She's sick of it.

> Hannah: *Joe, I need to talk to you about something important.*
>
> Joe: *Now, Hannah? Do we have to talk now?*
>
> Hannah: *Yes, It's really important.*
>
> Joe: *Look I just have to finish this shelf I'm repairing. I'll be with you in about ten minutes, OK?*
>
> Hannah: *OK.*
>
> Joe (about twenty-seven minutes later): *OK to talk?*
>
> Hannah: Sure. (Hannah sits on the lounge and waits while Joe makes a cup of tea, just the way she likes it.) *Thanks.*

Joe (Looks her in the eye): *Now what did you want to talk to me about?*

Hannah: *Well …* (tears well up, Joe stays silent, looking at her intently) … *I'm sorry to bring this up again but … .*

Joe: *No, it's OK. What is it?*

Hannah: *I got really hurt last night when you came home late … again … and you knew we were having friends over.* (long pause) *I had to entertain them, and make excuses for you.* (pause) *Alone. I entertained them … I talked … I didn't know whether to serve dinner or wait.*

Joe: *A-huh.*

Hannah: *I phoned, I reminded you, you said you'd be a few minutes. Then a few minutes turn into an hour and I was left making stupid small talk. Max feels uncomfortable when you're not around, Ellie wanted to have a good chat, but with Max hanging around she just made stupid small talk, and we talked about how late you were, and I was afraid to put the rice on and that desert would melt and I … I …*

Joe: *How did it make you feel?*

Hannah: *Angry!! I felt really angry Joe! And Hurt. Alone. Like you don't want to be with me. I mean. I know that's not true, that things just come up, but they always come up, and I just have to understand that, but it hurts!*

Joe: *You felt angry and hurt.*

Hannah: <u>*And*</u> *alone* <u>*and*</u> *abandoned. By you.*

Joe: *Alone and abandoned too, huh?*

Hannah: *By you.*

Joe: *By me.*

Hannah: *Yes. I mean, sure, I know you Joe, I know you don't mean it. You're just like that. You get involved in whatever's in front of you, or you miscalculate the traffic, or something. Whatever. But it's always the same and I'm sick of it.*

Joe: *A-huh.*

Hannah: *I'm sick of talking to our friends without you, or waiting for you to arrive home, or waiting in airports and bus stations, or just hoping you won't be too late this time. I hate it. I get embarrassed because I worry what other people think.*

Joe: *You get embarrassed and worry what others think.*

Hannah: *You know I do. It's just gotten too much.*

Joe: *A-huh.*

Hannah: *And I'm sick of making excuses.*

Joe: *A-huh.* (after a silence) *Is there anything else you wanted to tell me?*

Hannah (after a long silence): *I want you to try harder.*

Joe: *You want me to try harder.*

Hannah: *Yes.*

Joe: (silent)

Hannah: *I do.*

Joe (after another pause): *Anything else?*

Hannah: *No. That's about it.*

Joe: *A-huh.* (more silence) *So, this … this late thing of mine has gotten to you too much, … you get so sick of it … you feel so hurt and angry, embarrassed, and all that, that you had to … what?*

Hannah: *Make sure you understood.* (pause) *And ask you to try harder.*

Joe (after a pause): *OK.*

Hannah (after some silence): *You OK I said that?*

Joe (with a caring smile): *Sure. … You know I can't promise anything.*

Hannah: *I know. But you could try.*

Joe: *I could.* (hugs Hannah)

This small interchange has all the hallmarks of a good listening session. For all his faults, I've made Joe a pretty good listener. (Hannah likes that).

So, let's go through it to see where Joe got it right.

Joe got it right with Hannah even though he'll still be late in the future. He's not stupid enough to make promises he can't keep, and Hannah knows this. This ended in a loving hug because Joe didn't get defensive and he didn't start attacking Hannah. It was hard for him, but he just listened.

The listening brought out the love.

1. Joe followed the <u>listening EARS roadmap</u>. He established an environment to encourage listening by making a time to sit down with Hannah in their comfy lounge, make her a cup of tea, and look her in the eye. They were alone and wouldn't be disturbed. He wasn't distracted; he was there for her. Then the listening began.

Joe kept asking questions and interjected only with *A-huh* occasionally. He used silence a lot. This can be as good as asking a question because it leaves space for the talker. This way, Hannah spoke about 80% of the time, or more.

He often repeated back words that Hannah had used. This let Hannah know that he was taking in what she was saying, without him changing stuff in his own mind. You will notice at one stage Hannah noticed that Joe didn't use <u>all</u> of her words, and she corrected him (several times):

> Hannah: *I felt really angry Joe! Hurt. Alone. Like you don't want to be with me. I mean. I know that's not true, that things just come up, but they always come up, and I just have to understand that, but it hurts!*
>
> Joe: *You felt angry and hurt.*

Hannah: *<u>And</u> alone and abandoned. By you.*

Joe: *Alone and abandoned too, huh?*

Hannah: *By you.*

Joe: *By me.*

But that's OK. Joe is allowed to make mistakes; that's part of listening.

Joe could feel the listening session was coming to an end so he summarized the situation:

Joe: *A-huh. (more silence) So, this ... this late thing of mine has gotten to you too much ... you get so sick of it ... you feel so hurt and angry, embarrassed, and all that, that you had to ... what?*

Hannah: *Make sure you understood. (pause) And ask you to try harder.*

Joe (after a pause): *OK.*

He checked that there wasn't anything else she needed to tell him with:

Joe (after another pause): *Anything else?*

At that point, Hannah would have been free to launch into a tirade: *Yeah, and that's another thing, you always look creased and crumpled by the end of the day, you could at least come home to freshen-up and put something more decent on, you know, to look relaxed and ready to be with friends.* But she didn't. She left that for another day. (Phew.)

If Joe had done nothing else right, but just stuck to the EARS formula as he did, it would have gone well. But he did better. He applied the other five basics of listening. Here's what he did.

2. <u>Being there.</u> He was there for Hannah. Making the cup of tea was being there. (Hannah loves tea in her favourite yellow cup with a picture of their son on it. Joe knows this.) Looking someone in the eyes always says you are there for them, (but intense eye contact may not always be appropriate).

3. <u>One-way street.</u> Joe left lots of silence. Silence says *this is not a conversation, it is a one-way street, the space is there for you to take up.* Joe could have turned it into a conversation with things like *yeah, well you aren't exactly perfect Hannah* or he could have turned it into an argument with *listen, I work damn hard to give you this lifestyle … .* Fortunately he didn't. Hannah did most of the talking, and most of the silences were controlled by her. This also shows it's a listening session, not a conversation.

4. <u>Shelving beliefs.</u> Joe didn't get defensive and he didn't attack Hannah. This showed that he shelved his beliefs. It's hard to hear a criticism, even given gently as Hannah did. But Joe didn't waiver. He kept his opinions to himself.

5. <u>Not problem-solving</u>. There was just a little problem-solving in Joe's undertaking to "try," but that was it. It was almost all listening. The bottom line is that this problem is not likely to be solved. Feelings-based conversation helps keep problem-solving away. Joe asked *how did that make you feel?* in contrast to *you want to know what I think?* which leads to problem-solving.

6. <u>Engendering trust</u>. The listening session took a lot of trust. Hannah had to trust that Joe would take criticism, Joe had to trust Hannah wouldn't criticize him too harshly. Hannah showed her vulnerability: *I get embarrassed because I worry what other people think.* Hannah had to trust that Joe wouldn't hit her with *well you think too much about appearances, who cares what others think?* She was vulnerable to attack. She trusted Joe, and he respected that trust.

Thank you Joe. Somewhere along the line, he learnt the skill of listening. He used the listening EARS roadmap and the six basics of listening to deepen his understanding of Hannah. Their relationship is the real winner.

But he still turns up late. (It's a problem yet to be solved.)

CHAPTER TWO

Practicing Listening

Ok, so now you know the basics. In this chapter, I'll take you through practicing the skill of listening, step by step. Having been a professional classical musician, I know some things about listening; deep listening. As a psychiatrist, I know how to apply this to people. We'll start off by doing things you can do on your own: listening to sounds around you, listening to music, and listening at the theatre or the movies. Then we'll move on to listening to people. As crazy as it may sound, in this image saturated, immediate gratification world, many of us have forgotten how to <u>really</u> listen to nature and music.

I'm going to take you through an active listening course in half a dozen or so easy exercises. Through this, you will safely and proficiently learn and practice the core listening skills. In this chapter, you will learn to …

> ***listen to nature for details,***
> ***listen to music for meanings,***
> ***listen at the theatre for empathy,***
> ***and practice with people.***

Ready? Let's go.

Practicing listening

Practice is practice, work is work, effort is effort. You will only get good at a skill if you practice it. You will go through periods of *I'm not good at this … I don't get it*, but also periods of *I'm starting to get the hang of this … hey, this is worth it, I'm getting better!* You will reap the rewards in your relationships: people will like and trust you more.

THM: Any skill takes practice.

It can be daunting to launch into practicing with a real person. Eventually, however, you are going to do that. The beauty of the approach here is to get you started with sounds around you and with music. Nature sounds or music won't complain if you get something wrong. But remember, you're allowed to make mistakes in listening. It's OK. The only real mistake you are not allowed to make in active listening is abandoning the person by walking away; or outright insulting them. Just by being there and trying, you're doing it, and letting the other person know you care.

Listening to sounds around you for details

You can <u>hear</u> the sounds around you. Some of us even <u>listen</u> to the sounds around us. Now you will <u>actively listen</u> to the sounds around you.

What's the difference? Let's recap from Chapter One.

<u>Hearing</u> is the registration of physical sounds in your brain with help from your ears.

<u>Listening</u> is paying some attention and attaching some meaning to the sounds.

<u>Active listening</u> is more attention, focus and concentration. You exclude everything except the sound you want. Your feelings are open to being moved, and your thoughts are making connections. You are engaged with your whole being.

Whether in a bustling city or in tranquil nature, the world is full of sounds. Often, we are not aware of the things we can hear. As soon as you ask yourself, *oh, wait a minute, what's that?* you are listening.

Try these simple exercises, right now, wherever you are.

EXERCISE ONE: LISTENING FOR NATURE

Stop! Can you hear any sound of nature?

Oh, wait a minute, I do hear rushing water / a bird / wind in the trees.

Good, now you're listening. Stand still and quite. Listen more.

How does the sound make you feel?

What do you mean? Oh, I see, it's a hot day and the sound relaxes me. It makes me feel good. Peaceful. I smile. In fact, I wonder about that water / a bird / wind …

Now you're active-listening.

EXERCISE TWO: LISTENING FOR MECHANICAL SOUNDS

Hey! Can you hear the traffic or a jet plane?

What, are you crazy? Of course I can, I can't get away from it!!

Just listen to it.

Horns, squeaky brakes, accelerating cars, noisy trucks (or whatever you hear).

Good. Now actively listen; go deeper.

To that racket?? OK. … petrol engines … that one's a diesel … that guy's angry, I can tell by the way he's on the horn … rush hour … I'm glad I'm walking. (Or whatever you think and feel about what you heard).

You can do these exercises anywhere at any time and it will improve your listening skills.

THM: *Hear. Then listen. Then actively listen to sounds anywhere at any time.*

Hearing is just hearing. In listening, you walk alongside the sound for a while. When you actively listen, you open yourself up in a much fuller way.

As I type this, I am at a public swimming pool in an airport. I hear children playing in the water, jumbo jets revving their engines, fleeting conversations in English and other languages, occasional take-offs, and the sounds of little plastic wheels as people pass me schlepping around their luggage.

Just to write the preceding paragraph, I had to listen to the sounds for a while: single them out and label them. I walked beside them just long enough to identify them and give them a name.

Now, I will actively listen to one of the sounds. The children. There must be about four kids aged about six or seven. Their playful splashing about makes me smile. They remind me of my own kids when they were young. I grow sad as I realize that time when my kids were small is never coming back. Perhaps grand-children one day. Now I shift my focus to the jets. The sheer power of a jet engine excites me. (I'm a bit of a rev-head.) Then the sounds of schlepped baggage wheels make me feel weary.

This is active listening: being with the sounds in a close, intimate way. Letting sounds affect my thoughts and feelings and allowing them to change my inner world. Hearing usually doesn't change your inner world.

Listen to your world. Let the sounds affect your thoughts and feelings and let them change your inner world. Remember these experiences. One day, they will help you "walk beside" someone you are listening to.

Just now, I hear a jumbo jet take-off. I listen. There is a strange vibration in one engine, … it is smooth again, … the engine finds its rhythm and the plane accelerates down the runway. The sound becomes feint … it is gone.

I could not direct the sound at all. My mind flowed wherever the sound led me. It took me and I followed. Let the sounds of the world lead you. Remember this when it comes to listening to people. Let their sounds lead you.

The distant jumbo jet made me feel lonely, because my loved ones are far away, yet excited as I think about the miracle of flight and re-joining them.

An array of emotions and curious thoughts are aroused through active listening. This creates beautiful moments. If you don't take the time to listen, and actively listen, you will miss these moments.

THM: Actively listen to open yourself to a whole world of beautiful moments.

Take time. Actively listen to sounds around you. Whether you are in the hustle and bustle of a big city or are able to experience the subtle nature sounds of birds, bees and wind in the trees. Listen.

EXERCISE THREE: LISTENING IN NATURE

Get out in nature. Find a spot to relax and be undisturbed. Take a decent chunk of time, at least an hour. Lie on the grass, sit on a bench, on sand or wherever. Look around to familiarise yourself with nature's wonder. Take a few deep breathes. Relax.

Then close your eyes and just listen.

Hear; then listen; then actively listen. Open up your thoughts and feelings and allow the sounds, however short or quiet, to affect your inner world.

Ask yourself these questions.

> *What is that sound?*
> *Why is it happening now?*
> *What does it remind me of?*
> *What emotions does it evoke in me?*
> *What other thoughts does the sound lead me to?*

Move on to another sound and follow through the same questions. There may be four or five dominant sounds around you. Listen to silence as well, and work through the same questions.

Do this task in a nature location. Find a space, have some time, and have a willingness to listen. The experience can do wonders.

Learning to actively listen to nature sounds lays the groundwork for deep listening to another human being: you just have to be there, sounds come at you, there is nothing to judge, there is no problem to solve, and you cultivate warm feelings of trust just by being in nature. These are the basics of listening. The only thing you don't practice in nature is the listening EARS roadmap.

In nature, sounds tend to be random, even chaotic. Organised sounds begin to have more meaning; they become something else, like music.

Listening to music for meaning

Most of us listen to music: classical, jazz, rap, pop, rhythm and blues, rock, and so forth. Your taste in music doesn't matter. The many musical styles attest to the great diversity of people. Some people have a wide range of musical taste. (I know some people who like Country <u>and</u> Western).

But who <u>really</u> listens to music? If music is in the background, you are only hearing it. The challenge is to listen to it deeply, to listen to it actively.

It surprised me when I spent some time overseas, that many of my European friends would listen to English songs without understanding a single word. Then I realised that many people who understand English don't actually listen to the words either! They hear them, but they don't <u>listen</u> to them. This is because music itself can make us feel good. You don't have to understand the words to enjoy the music.

Let's use a popular song as an example of how to cultivate deeper, active listening.

Hearing Art Garfunkel's voice on the original recording of Paul Simon's *Bridge over Troubled Water* gives us an emotional experience regardless of whether or not we listen to or understand the words. The song is about sacrificial love. The music itself conveys the powerful emotion of sacrificial love. The words have Christ-like allusions. The gospel style of piano playing reinforces these allusions.

Once you listen to the words and become aware of the allusions, you have more understanding of the song's power. Art's voice seems to cry out in caring desperation. The melody touches you more, paving the way for a deeper music-listening experience. When your head understands, and your heart is open, you can feel more.

THM: *The head and the heart work together in listening to music, and to people.*

When you understand what some of the different instruments are doing, you can go further. Drums, for example, drive through your whole body in a physical, visceral sensation that often defies words. The bass guitar often works together with drums to lay down a solid rhythm for a song. The keyboards and guitars sometimes play rhythmic patterns or launch into solos or counter-melodies to enhance or dance around a vocal line.

The melodic line of a song often expresses the words. In the chorus, for example, the words *like a bridge over troubled water*, are sung in a melodic line that descends from above, like a high bridge laying itself down over troubled waters. The melody paints the picture conveyed by the words. To gain this insight, you have to listen actively.

In the original recording of *Bridge over Troubled Water*, the drummer pounded a large steel chain on the bathroom floor of the recording studio. This sound gives a sense of epic proportions to the song when the sound starts and grows louder. The same sound is used in *The Boxer* on the same album to express the painful blows the boxer receives as he fights other fighters and tries to make ends meet in a difficult life.

I've shared these things with you not to flaunt my knowledge, but to whet your curiosity about active listening in music.

Go deeper. Just like listening to the sounds around you, you can hear music, listen to music, or listen actively. Nearly every piece of music will reveal deeper emotional states to you if you can actively listen to it. You don't have to intellectually understand what happens in the music (although understanding helps a lot), just be emotionally open to listen to what the words <u>may</u> mean and the music <u>may</u> be expressing.

When you think about how the melody line or the sounds may reflect the words, you are linking your head and your heart. There is no right or wrong in this, just a deeper experience.

Nature sounds, as I mentioned, are not organized. Music is organized. Someone put it together with an intention in mind. This gives it a meaning or a specific set of meanings waiting to be discovered. Music has meanings independent of whoever put the music together. All music has a life of its own. Because of this, one very important question arises as you listen to it. It begs an answer only discovered by active listening.

What does the music mean to me?

The answer may be different for every person. Whenever you listen to music it's like it's just you and the music, there is no one else. That makes it a unique experience for everyone; a unique meaning made from the music and your unique responses to it.

The music + my responses = a unique meaning.

Remember this when listening with people. Every listening session with a person becomes a unique event; a combination of what the talker is saying and how you receive their message. Their words will be unique; your responses will be unique. This uniqueness becomes one of the reasons listening builds trust.

The talker's message + my listening response = a unique meaningful experience.

Any shared experience builds trust, particularly if that experience is unique and special.

THM: Every listening encounter is unique and special.

I once stood on a beach and, on a memorial plaque, I read the story of a shipwreck over a hundred years ago. A man and a woman helped each other to survive the frightening experience. They were strangers to each other and they were the only survivors. It was no surprise to learn that the couple later married. I imagine that immense trust would have built up between the two of them: through the storm, the wreck, the seas, finding each other, being washed ashore, days on the beach, then weeks before returning home. They were alone and together in a unique and intense experience, never to be forgotten.

EXERCISE FOUR: LISTENING TO MUSIC

Find a quiet room where you can be alone. Again, give yourself a decent chunk of time; at least an hour. Lie down on the floor or sink into a sofa. Use headphones if you like. Find the original *Bridge over Troubled Water* album by Simon and Garfunkel, and listen to the title track. Before you do, take a few deep breathes. Relax. Then close your eyes and just listen.

I have given you a few things to listen for. Listen for them. Listen to the words, Art's voice, the gospel feel of the piano, the unassuming way the bass guitar introduces itself, the steel chain recorded in the bathroom; and listen to the rousing, searing, and hopeful climax.

Actively listen.

You may want to listen to the track a few times. When you are familiar with this song, ask yourself the following questions.

> *What emotions does it evoke in me?*
> *What other thoughts does it lead me to?*
> *What are the different instruments doing?*
> *What do the words mean?*
> *How does the music enhance the meaning in the words?*
> *Why does the music get loud, soft, fast, slow, dramatic or peaceful?*

And the all-important music-listening question:

> *What does the music mean to me?*

You can then listen to *The Boxer* on the same album or to any other music: your favourite, some music you have never listened to, or some music you may not like. Actively listening to music regular to unwind, relax, learn, experience, and get in touch with your thoughts and feelings.

Listening at the theatre for empathy

Before we move on to listening with people, I want you to listen to a play at the theatre. *What!* I hear you saying. *The music stuff is alright, but now you want me to go to a play?*

Yes.

You can substitute listening to a movie if you want, but the live experience of a theatre play is far better. It is dynamic and changing where film is static. Nothing can go wrong with a film, and each "performance" is the same. Actors on stage will change their performances depending on how you, as an audience member, laugh, cry or applaud. Theatre is alive, just like the people you are practicing to listen to. Alive.

We normally go to <u>see</u> a play; but I want you to go to <u>listen</u> actively.

A play is almost custom-designed to have you listening actively. It is never in the background to just hear. The playwright has written a narrative (story) to draw you in to the action. The acting, directing, sets and costumes also draw you in. You actively listen.

Live people in flesh and blood in front of you on the stage draw you in emotionally. This is the feeling of empathy: you feel for the characters, with the characters, it is as though you go through what they go through. It is like they talk to you alone. You can feel their vulnerability. They pour their thoughts and emotions into their roles. This is very close to a one-on-one listening session. Empathy is having your emotions and thoughts open to the action, the characters, and the relationships among the characters. It is "walking alongside" the characters for a while.

The story and characters in the play will naturally bring up all sorts of emotions in you. Theatre does that. It's time to go to the theatre.

EXERCISE FIVE: THEATRE LISTENING

Choose a play, decide on a performance, ask a friend along, book tickets and go. It doesn't matter if it's a professional or a school production, the process of listening is the same. Enjoy the evening. Sometime after the performance, work through the following empathy questions.

> *How would I feel or react in that character's situation?*
> *How would I feel if that character was talking to me?*
> *How am I like that character?*
> *How am I different?*

These questions are designed to help you empathize with the characters; to think and feel yourself into the situation of the character; to see something of yourself in them. We naturally empathize with each other because we are all human beings.

THM: *We naturally empathize with each other, if we let ourselves.*

Guess what I'm going to tell you? You guess it. Remember this experience when it comes to listening to people. But make sure you experience it when you go to the theatre.

The basis of empathy is feeling <u>with</u> someone. When you listen to someone, you not only walk beside them, you also feel with them and identify. You can ask yourself the following questions to help you feel with anyone you are listening to.

> *How would I feel or react in that person's situation?*
> *How do I feel now that the person is talking to me?*
> *How am I like this person?*
> *How am I different?*

When Joe was listening to Hannah, he allowed space for her feelings, he listened to her feelings, and he felt with her. He had empathy. He felt some of her pain as she told him how hard things were. This is active listening. He stayed with her and felt with her. This made Hannah feel close to Joe, and gave her the feeling that he really cares for her (which he does). If Hannah was a character on stage, and Joe was in the audience, he would be listening to her pain as the actor poured her emotions into the role onstage.

Listening at a play is very much like listening to real people.

Listening to people

OK. Now for the big step.

***THM: You've learnt to hear details by listening to nature.
You've learnt to listen for underlying meanings through music.
You've learnt to empathize by seeing a play or a movie.
Once you've practiced all these, you're ready for people.***

A listening interaction with a person is much more intense than any listening to nature, music or theatre. A person has feelings which can be hurt. Nature sounds, music and theatre productions won't be disappointed if you say something harsh or insensitive. They also have less of a need to be "heard."

Before you take on this challenge, let me remind you that even if you get every technique wrong, it doesn't matter. If you are there for them, then you are listening. Remember the only mistake you can really make is abandoning the person or outright insulting their feelings. By reading this book, I know you want to listen well. If you listened to nature, music and at the theatre, then you already do.

You, as a listener, also have feelings. This is where empathy comes in: you the listener, a human being, wonder what it is like to be the talker, another human being. What's it like to be in their position; in their shoes; to be treated like that? The aim is to treat them the way you would like to be treated: with care, respect and dignity.

If you are able to do this, you are listening.

THM: In listening, treat others the way you like to be treated.

Active listening to people is attentive and focussed. It involves listening for information, thoughts and feelings and being aware of how this affects your own thoughts and feelings. You are wholly engaged in the listening process.

You cannot direct the sounds of nature, music, or the theatre. Similarly, you are not going to direct a talker. You will allow them talk about what <u>they</u> want to talk about, and you will leave space for <u>them</u> to control the conversation.

When listening to nature sounds, you become aware of the depths of your own mind. Now, when listening to a person, become equally aware of the depths of their mind. This brings unique meaningful moments through active listening. Be curious about their thoughts and their feelings.

The diversity of music styles is a reminder of how diverse people are. If you do not like the "style" of the talker, you can still be fascinated and appreciative.

Just as you listened to music's different speeds, volumes and moods, you'll listen to different tones, speeds, and volumes in the talker's speech. "Match" the person you are listening to: slow down when they slow down, speak quietly when they speak quietly, and reflect their pace and demeanour.

Listen to their words, and the full implication of their words just as you did with words in music and at the theatre. Do their words match their mood and their tone of voice? What are they really trying to say? Is a leg or finger nervously twitching? How does this affect the meaning of their words?

Just as music together with your unique responses created a unique meaning, so too their words together with your unique responses will create a unique meaning. This shared unique meaning builds trust.

When listening, you have a live flesh-and-blood person in front you, just like in the theatre. You can feel their vulnerability. Be gentle and careful.

Characters in plays often have a hidden agenda or motivation underneath their words. What are the talker's emotions and motivations underneath their words? This person may not be direct. They may feel the need to hide something. That's OK. Just be aware of this.

What is the "story" this person is trying to get across to you? How does it fit into their broader life story? We experience life moment-to-moment as well as decade-by-decade.

Ask yourself: *How would I feel in this person's situation? Can I empathize with them? Can I feel some of their pain or joy with them?*

OK. That's a long list of active listening lessons. But don't worry. This list is on the page in black and white for you to refer to whenever you need to. Revision is part of learning any new skill. For now, however, I want you to forget them all.

That's right. Forget them.

Don't have any of these things going through your mind while you are listening to someone. It's too much. It'll get in the way. If they're talking and your thinking about these techniques, then YOU'RE NOT LISTENING!!

So forget them. But continue to practice them. With practice these ideas will drop into your mind automatically. It's osmosis. Magic. (No, it's actually repeat practice of a skill and reading over and over.)

In listening to people, practice the six basics of listening.

1. The listening EARS roadmap
2. Listening is "being there" for the other person
3. Listening is not a conversation, it is a one-way street
4. Listening means shelving your beliefs and judgments
5. Listening is not problem-solving, and
6. Listening engenders trust.

Revise these basic principles often.

THM: Know the basics.

EXERCISE SIX: ROLE PLAY

The way to practice with people at first is through "role play." You take on the role of listener, and you find someone to be the talker. Using the EARS roadmap, listen as the talker talks about their real-life experiences based on the following settings.

1. Tell me about a difficult situation you had as a child at school.

2. Tell me about a difficult situation you have been in at work.

3. Did you ever have a pet die on you? How did you handle that?

4. Is there someone in your life you are having difficulties with? How are you handling it?

5. Tell me about a personal habit you have changed or would really like to change.

6. Tell me about someone in your life who has a different religious or political belief to you. How do you handle that situation?

Practice these with someone who knows you are learning. Your aim is to get through the session without getting frazzled. A practice listening session may last about five to ten minutes. You will need to use the six basics of listening.

1. <u>Listening EARS roadmap</u>. I'll give you some suggested phrases to use. Feel free to use them or not. Ultimately, use your words to

make these phrases sound naturally yours.

E: Opening questions after making sure you are both comfort-
able and private:
What did you want to talk about?
OK. What's on your mind?
You wanted to talk?
Are you OK?

A: *And then what happened?*
How did that make you feel?
So, then … (an invitation to keep talking)
Is there anything more you want to tell me?
How come … ?
Was there any particular reason you …?

R: Well, I can't write anything here can I.
Just repeat what your talker says back to you and make it
sound natural and sincere.

S: To summarize the situation, it can be helpful to have a little
formula that you practice until it sounds natural. Your
formula could include

So you needed to tell me that … and you felt … is that right?
Or
*Thanks for sharing that. I think I've got the picture. You felt
… about …? Anything else you wanted to talk about?*

Remember if you summarize too soon, and get it wrong, it's OK, the talker will let you know. Then ask just more questions, repeat what they say, and summarize again a bit later.

2. <u>Be there</u> by keeping interested and showing you are interested. Keep your eyes turned towards the talker, but break eye contact occasionally. Be sensitive to the amount of eye contact they do or don't want. Don't let your eyes wander, don't read a paper, just listen.

3. <u>Keep it a one-way street</u> by encouraging them to talk about 80% of the time. If the talker doesn't want to talk much, they are shy, the subject matter is difficult or they're letting you direct conversation. It's OK just to sit there in silence. After all, they want to talk to you, you are there to listen.

4. <u>Shelve your beliefs and judgments.</u> The more you practice, the more your brain will go into "listening mode." This includes shelving your beliefs and opinions. It is a skill and a habit your brain gets into. At first, however, you will battle having to do this. That's OK. You do not need to change your beliefs to listen. Just listen.

5. <u>Avoid problem-solving</u>, by not giving advice. If someone asks you for advice, say something like *I don't know the situation as well as you do; I can't imagine the right way forward. I'm here to listen*. If they want to explore problem-solving options with you, that's OK, but know that the listening session is over. Summarize

before moving to problem-solving. With some people, like your children or partner, it is your duty to help them problem-solve. That's fine; but remember that when you are problem-solving, you are in a new role.

6. <u>Build trust</u> by having good eye contact, a calm facial expression, a calm tone of voice, and by having an open body posture (don't have your arms and legs crossed and don't leaning forward threateningly). Eye contact and smiles engender trust, particularly with people you care about. "Match" the talker's volume, tone and pace to build trust. (We talk more about trust, eye contact and body posture in Chapter Four.)

Mostly, however, be yourself. This builds the most trust. Don't pretend to be someone you're not. Don't let techniques get in the way. The talker is being vulnerable by talking to you; you need to match this by being yourself. You do this by dropping the usual social mask we all have – just a little – and have the guts to let them see you are a human being, just like they are. That <u>really</u> builds trust.

That's why I want you to forget all techniques while listening to someone talk except the listening EARS roadmap. You listen well when you are being yourself.

THM: Always be yourself.

After you've finished a role-play session, ask the talker for feedback on how you the listener went.

How did that feel for you?
Did you feel like I was listening to you?
What did I do well?
What could I improve?

EXERCISE SEVEN: LISTENING IN CASUAL CONVERSATION

While you still doing role plays, start listening more and talking less in casual conversations. This is easier than you may think. You already do it to some extent anyway, right? Now you are going to do it more. If someone notices you being quiet and says something like *you're being funny ... why are you different?* Simply say *I'm working on becoming a better listener.* What are they going to say? *That's stupid! Don't! How dare you!!* No. If they say so or not, they will appreciate it.

Remember that listening is a gift you give another person.

THM: Listening is a gift.

In casual conversation, practice being interested in topics you may not usually be interested in. Ask questions, leave more space for others to talk, and let others explain things to you. The following questions are examples. You can use them at a bar, a dinner-party, anywhere.

I don't understand, what does a quarter-back do?
Can you tell me your views about the economy?

Could you explain to me why you believe that? I'm interested.

Try not to direct or control conversation too much – asking too many questions can do this – just listen and be interested. Listen to how conversation develops and flows. Be an observer. Just listen.

Listen to your friends, your work peers, and your family. Listen. Use the techniques, then forget the techniques, and be yourself. It's all helpful. The worst case scenario is that you will listen about the same as you did before. But that's unlikely.

Summary

Gradually you are becoming a better active listener. Practice listening to nature sounds for details, to music for underlying meanings, and at the theatre to empathize. These experiences enrich your life, provoke your thoughts, and move your feelings. They show you how to go with the flow, tolerate different styles, and they teach you about people's vulnerability and motivations. Take these skills across to listening to people in role play and casual conversation. Think about matching the other person, about unique meanings created, about trust, stories, and OK-ness.

Be yourself. Mistakes don't matter. We all make mistakes. Just keep listening to friends, family, work colleagues, clients and even strangers. Your life, and theirs, will be enriched.

CHAPTER THREE

Listening to your love-partner

You are now equipped with the listening EARS roadmap and the six basics from Chapter One. From Chapter Two you are equipped with listening for detail in nature, for unique meanings in music and empathizing in theatre. You can apply these insights and skills to listen in any situation. Listening to your love-partner is, however, a special case. This is the person you have a special connection with; a connection like no other. If you do not have a person like this in your life presently, chances are you want one. Listening can help you make a connection when the time is right for one.

Any lesson you learn in listening deeply to your love-partner will help you listen to anybody else in any other situation.

THM: Lessons learned in listening to you love-partner help in listening to anybody.

Listening to your love-partner is, for various reasons, more difficult than listening to anyone else. You want to equalize with this person the most, so taking the subservient listening role is a challenge. You want to share your beliefs and opinions with this person the most, so shelving them is a challenge. You have more problem-solving conversations with this person, so just to listen is a challenge. Yet this is the person you want to "be there" for the most and, ideally, this is the person you trust the most. You do not want to lose them, so sometimes you wonder if you can be totally honest with them and allow them to be totally honest with you.

The stakes are high.

Before you back away from the apparently daunting task of listening deeply to your love-partner, and have them listen deeply to you, keep in mind the following.

> *A relationship means sharing love, and having someone who knows and understands you.*
>
> *If you feel misunderstood by everyone, but your love-partner understands you; life is OK.*
>
> *If you feel abandoned by everyone, but your love-partner accepts you; life is pretty good.*
>
> *If you feel betrayed, hated or cheated by everyone, but your love-partner stands by you, loves you and is faithful to you; life is great.*

Active listening helps create this special bond. It is worth every effort and it can lead to even deeper love and understanding. So let's nurture this important relationship with listening.

Listening to your love-partner

Sharing your life with someone calls for adjustments: you don't get your way all the time, you don't always agree, you have differing strengths and weaknesses, and differing opinions. Often, your love-partner will need to share with you their requests, wishes, demands or criticisms. Hannah was criticising Joe about his lateness and demanding he try to do something about it. This was reasonable. Joe was asked to listen to something that was hard to hear. He did. The love he showed Hannah was in the listening and the trying; not in changing himself.

THM: The love is in the listening and the trying.

Listening to your love-partner is easy because you love them, but a challenge because of your own needs and demands. Your needs and demands work against the "one-way street" ideal of listening. The bottom line is that, when listening to your love-partner, you need to suspend your beliefs and judgments <u>and</u> your needs and demands. Just for the listening session. This is not easy.

THM: Listening to your love-partner means suspending your needs and demands as well.

Resentment builds up if one person is constantly adjusting and changing to accommodate the other. Listening ensures that resentment gets expressed and accepted, rather than bottled up. Listening allows constructive expression of feelings. Through listening you can know where you stand with your partner.

Talking things through and active listening is always healthy, as long as you can be gentle with each other.

THM: Be gentle with each other.

Remember that listening is a gift of love; a way of saying *I love you.*

THM: Listening says I love you.

Different domestic dialogues

Your love-partner is someone with whom you are in constant communication. Even if you are apart for a time, you tend still to have an inner awareness of what they may be doing, and communication may be via phone or the internet. Let's categorize the times you spend together and the different ways you may dialogue. Knowing there are different dialogues will help you plan for listening times when you need them.

<u>On the fly</u>. On the fly dialogue happens anywhere and anytime during the demands of day-to-day life. Things need to be said and information needs to be exchanged quickly. Both people may be talking and listening. There is little if any active listening.

<u>Down time</u>. Down time talk, during breaks, televisions shows, quiet reading times and games, may be relaxing banter or just to

share something interesting. This type of dialogue is usually kept light, playful and humorous.

On the fly and down-time dialoguing makes up much of our relationship interactions. They are laden with meaning but are not necessarily goal directed. The following domestic dialogues, however, have specific meanings and objectives.

<u>Having a conversation</u>. A conversation is a more focussed form of dialogue. It may happen during the day, during a drive, a walk, while doing chores, after love-making, before sleep or over a cup of tea, coffee, or wine. Conversation is a two-way, give-and-take process that is mutually satisfying. Both people are being and sharing themselves. Talking and listening naturally alternate. Topics for discussions may include the relationship, work issues, future dreams, others, or any topic of interest. It is a specific time of sharing.

<u>Problem-solving</u>. This is dialogue with purpose; a definite goal. A couple may need to talk through a relationship, parenting, financial, social or work-related issue to come to an understanding or reach a solution. This is important in the lives of all couples. Problem-solving sessions often may follow listening sessions (or argument sessions, or not-talking sessions) or become part of any conversation.

<u>Romance and flirting</u>. Couples may develop a pet language that only they share, they may flirt with each other, or speak out intimacies during tender moments. This is a very private form of communication and affirms the love bond.

<u>Arguing</u>. Conflict is virtually inevitable when two fully thinking, feeling, autonomous human beings live together. Handling this conflict in a relationship is not easy. An argument is a dialogue that confronts conflicts and expresses thoughts and feelings. It is usually goal directed but not always constructive. Many people feel anger and hurt in arguments, but at least in arguments a couple is still in relationship.

An argument can be a good prelude to a listening session:

> *Do you want to sit down and talk about what that was all about? I'll listen to your side of things first.*

<u>The silent treatment</u>. Not talking is just a form of wordless arguing at a distance; emotions are usually still flared up. It is avoiding rather than confronting the conflict. The conflict is, however, still felt. Emotions, thoughts and feelings get suppressed rather than expressed. If you are "not talking" you are still communicating: watching behaviours, body language, looking for signs of diplomatic envoys or olive branches, seeing if things have gone "too far" this time, and so forth. Communication is through body language, behaviours and expressions more than through words.

A period of not talking can also be a good prelude to a listening session:

> *Do you want to sit down and talk about what that was all about? I'll listen to your side of things first.*

<u>Listening sessions</u>. Listening sessions are times when one person has a particular burden that they need to share with the other. (Like Hannah needing to share her frustration with Joe.) Listening sessions often precede problem-solving, but – for the purposes of this book – I am encouraging you to keep them separate. They can be an intense and intimate form of dialogue.

It is wise, as the talker, to speak out your needs during a listening session. That's good communication. You could, for example, flag your need to have a listening session with the following.

> *I need to talk to you; do you have a minute?*
> *I need you to be gentle while I share something.*
> *I need you to listen for a bit.*

Sometimes a talker is not that clear. You, the listener, may need to ask a question to make sure this is (or isn't) a listening session. This is good communication.

> *Are we having a conversation or a listening session?*
> *Do you want my opinion on this?*
> *Do you need me to problem-solve or just listen?*

THM: Ask "is this is a listening or problem-solving session?"

Then, as you listen, go through the six basics.

> 1. Listening EARS roadmap
> 2. Be there

3. Keep it a one-way street
4. Shelve your beliefs and judgments (and your demands and needs)
5. Avoid problem-solving, and
6. Build trust.

Keep quiet about your own needs and demands, particularly if your love-partner is saying something which is hard for you to hear. Their opinion matters. Sure, they can hurt you like no-one else can. They can also love you like no-one else can. That is why the stakes are so high. The relationship matters.

You feel the need to be equal with them. *It's not fair if they get to criticize me without me criticizing them! They don't understand!* You need to suspend your judgments and needs while you are the listener. This is really difficult to do. I still find it very difficult. I often fail. But your turn will come. Wait. Otherwise there is no progress and the listening session will move into a conversation or an argument.

THM: In a relationship the need to equalize is strong, work hard to suspend your beliefs and needs while you listen.

Underlying many relationship interactions (or lack of interactions) is fear of loss of the relationship. Ideally, you know that your relationship is strong enough to survive whatever needs to be said in a listening session. But, at the start of a relationship, there are times when the relationship will not survive. Some things <u>do</u> mean goodbye. Each of us still carry around a remnant of this fear from the early relationship; this vulnerability. So be gentle as the talker and as the listener. As the listener, your job is to make it as safe as possible for the talker to say whatever they need to. Hopefully, they will be gentle in what they say.

THM: The stakes are high, so remember to make it safe to share.

The talker also wants you to be your authentic self, not some phoney using techniques. (My love-partner gets very insulted if I <u>ever</u> forget to be my true self.) Yet they want you to be a good listener, and this means using the skills. If they complain about this complexity while you are learning to listen well, say *I'm just trying to do what that stupid shrink says in that book so I can be a better listener for you!* Again, what are they going to say? They can only say thank you for your consideration and effort. Listening is, after all, an act of love.

As you practice, you will be more of your authentic self. All in all, however, being yourself will always trump using techniques when it comes to your love-partner. They want the real you.

THM: Be your true self in relating to your love-partner.

Congratulations. That's it. That's all you need to remember to listen well to your love-partner. You can still ask for feedback while you learn the skill of listening (see Chapter Two). Before we move on, however, let's face some difficult issues.

Listening to difficult issues

At times, your love-partner will need to express certain difficult things. They may, for example, feel the need to criticize you, discuss sexual intimacy, talk about their own weaknesses, or share an important idea they fear you may reject.

The stakes are even higher in these issues; remember that remnant feeling of *oh no, this could be the end of the relationship!* They can feel vulnerable, open to emotional attack, or losing you, your respect or approval. They need to trust that you will still accept them and their feelings, and that you will not be too hurt. Here's the conflict: they don't want to hurt or lose you, yet they have a need they want fulfilled. This conflict can be intense when all they want is harmony and peace.

You too want harmony and peace.

In this situation, many people opt not to share things: they don't criticize, talk about intimacy, talk about weaknesses, or share ideas that may be rejected. They avoid conflict to keep the peace. This is reasonable. The cost, however, is not being true to self, not getting the need met, ongoing inner turmoil, and forsaking the possibility of deeper love and understanding.

To keep the peace, thoughts and feelings get bottled up. A part of the person doesn't get expressed or lived out. It is withheld from their love-partner out of fear. For this reason, I always encourage people to share things, safely.

THM: *Keeping things bottled up comes at a high cost.*

Tragically, in couple's therapy I often get to hear about things both parties want to do but would never dare tell the other.

Sam: *Sometimes I wish I could leave my job and move to Hawaii. We used to talk about these things, but now it's only a dream, she'd never go for it.*

Sally: *Sometimes I wish he would have the courage to quit his job and whisk me off to Hawaii. We used to talk about it, but I would never put that pressure on him.*

Unless these guys get to some honest talking, they will never do what they both want.

This is the case in discussing sexual wants as well as in sharing future dreams. In couple's therapy it happens from time to time that both people want to engage in certain sexual expressions, but neither would dare tell the other. Deeper trust and sharing is missed. Listening can overcome this, just as it can get two people to Hawaii if that's what they both want.

To have a dream come true, you need to have a dream and share it with your love-partner. If your partner doesn't want that dream, then listening is still the best way of working through the conflict.

Openness can bring renewed vigour, deepened trust, and personal freedom:

I feel so free being able to talk to you about these things
I never thought I could share these things with you
I thought you would reject me, but now I know how much
you love me
I used to bottle things up
I was afraid you would lose respect for me
I can finally be myself
The arguments hurt, but at least I know where we stand
The truth hurts, but I find I can love you more
Knowing your weaknesses, means I can admit to mine
I can finally say goodbye to walking on egg-shells around
you

On and on the comments go. For me, seeing a couple reach this level of trust – particularly after decades of holding back – is rewarding.

Couples who reach this level of trust find deeper love. But each must feel safe enough to be able to share their inner thoughts and feelings. This means the courage to share thoughts and feelings, and the gentleness to listen with understanding and acceptance.

THM: The talker needs courage to share difficult issues. The listener needs to make it safe with understanding, acceptance and gentleness.

To help you listen to difficult issues, I want to introduce you to two helpful insights:

THM: Your love-partner <u>wants</u> to share their true feelings with you. You have the choice of hearing the truth, or remaining ignorant. Choose truth.

THM: If something difficult is being shared, your job is to listen.

When your love-partner shares something difficult with you, quickly your mind will go:

> *Oh no! they want me to change! I don't know if I can do it!! I'll fail! It's all over!*

Remember the vulnerability you needed to have as a listener. I spoke about it earlier. Well this is it. It's crunch time. Stay calm, you'll get through it.

Here's the good news. You don't actually need to change, although you may choose to try. Your immediate job is simply to listen. Listening engenders trust. The love is in the listening. And in the trying, if that is what you eventually choose to do. Now, choose to listen.

THM: Love is in the listening and the trying. You won't agree on everything.

Let's look at each of these difficult issues, and I'll give you some tips to help you shut up and listen: even though you may be screaming inside.

Hearing criticism

Many people believe they have no right to criticize others (yet they happily criticize those that criticize others). Part of being a couple is helping one another to become better people. Think of it in terms of teaching rather than criticizing and it'll make sense. Teaching can be done with love.

If I pick my nose in public, I would like my love-partner to (gently) point this out to me so that I can improve myself. If others avoid my partner because she dominates conversation, I have the opportunity to teach her. If my sarcastic sense of humour hurts my partner, I'd rather know about it. If I feel manipulated by her, it's best she knows about it.

Ooh, that hurts!

It may hurt at first, but teaching is always helpful. It lifts up where criticism tends to put down; it broadens knowledge rather than shutting down interactions. Teach your love-partner the best way to handle you. Teach your love-partner to become better. Who will do this for you if you don't do it for each other?

THM: It's OK to teach one another. Teaching lifts up, criticizing puts down.

Choose your words and tone carefully, and start with a question. You will get better results if you need to teach your partner something.

Criticizing: *Stop picking your nose! You're disgusting!*
Teaching: *Do you know you pick your nose in public?*

Criticizing: *Why don't you just shut up and let others talk!*
Teaching: *Do you know you dominated conversation tonight?*

Criticizing: *I hate your goddam sarcasm!*
Teaching: *Do you know how much your sarcasm hurts me?*

Criticizing: *You're manipulative! Stop it!!*
Teaching: *You know, I'm feeling manipulating by you.*

Some would say Hannah was criticizing Joe for his lateness. This was hard for Joe to hear. But she was trying to teach him to do something so that she did not get hurt, embarrassed or frustrated. A happier Hannah is good news for Joe. With good listening, Joe could hear, understand and accept what Hannah needed to say. This paves the way for Joe to try to improve. Teaching will help someone improve, criticizing puts them down. At no point did Hannah put Joe down. If nothing changes, Hannah and Joe are closer just because of the sharing that good listening brings.

That's the point. The love is in the listening. I'm going to say it again:

THM: The love is in the listening.

As a listener, your only job is to listen to their teaching (previously known as criticism). Calm down and listen. Don't become defensive and don't attack. If you defend or attack, you're not listening. Listen, accept and understand. Thank them for caring about you enough to teach you. This will help them to not criticize in anger but to teach in care. Afterwards you will be able to ponder some of these questions.

> *Why would someone who loves me tell me this?*
> *Is there truth in what they tell me?*
> *Can I agree with at least some of it?*
> *Can I better myself in any way?*

You may then need them to listen to how you see the situation. Do not, however, negate what they have said. Their feelings are always true. They can't be wrong about what they feel.

THM: Nobody can be wrong about their feelings.

Take a moment to think about this.

Listening to issues of sexual intimacy

Sexual intimacy is part of who we are as human beings. In a long-term relationship, sexual expression is entwined with feelings of love and acceptance. Expectations can be high, and disappointments can bring despair. But listening well can help ameliorate this.

For most people, intimacy, in a way, defines a long-term

relationship. It is something shared with this one person only. In having to talk about complaints, wants or needs regarding sexual intimacy, the risk of rejection, disappointment or conflict is always there. So many people put up with less-than-satisfying intimacy to keep the peace. They avoid conflict.

The answer, again, is for the talker to find the courage to speak gently and the listener to make it safe by listening gently. The listener needs to be non-judgmental, accepting, and under-standing to build trust. The love is in the listening. Even a difficult listening session can be a unique meaningful expression of intimacy, like love-making itself.

THM: Listening can be an intimate act of love.

Assure the talker that you will listen and that it's OK for them to say what they are feeling. It is, even if you are more than a little nervy. Thank them for trusting you. Keep affirming your love. Remember the worst outcome is that nothing changes, you have heard the truth, and love has been shared. (It may not always feel that good though). Afterwards, there may be a problem-solving session to help plan for more satisfying sexual expression.

You may feel hurt about something they have just said to you. As a listener; hold on to the discomfort until it is your turn to talk and theirs to listen.

Because this is an emotionally charged area, listening sessions quickly move to problem-solving or alternating listening sessions: I *talk, you listen, then you talk, I listen.* Holding hands and other touches at key times help keep the loving connection alive. Touches always say *I care.*

THM: Touches during listening say "I'm here and I care."

After listening in the area of sexual intimacy, it will take time for anyone to digest what was said. Change may be more difficult. Professional help may be needed, even for the listening.

Listening to someone's weaknesses

It is easy to admit to our strengths but difficult to own up to weaknesses. Discussing weaknesses is complex:

What if I'm rejected?
What if I'm not the wonderful person they thought I was?

Fear of rejection and fear of losing respect is strong. But it goes deeper.

I can't accept my own fear, cowardice, guilt, selfishness or manipulation, so how can I expect them to?
I <u>hate</u> this part of me and try to hide it, so why should I share it?
How could anyone accept this? I don't!

It is important to listen compassionately when anyone is sharing their weaknesses with you, but particularly your love-partner.

Our weaknesses can bring up intense feelings of shame. To keep the peace, it often seems easier to bury it. But we <u>all</u> have weaknesses, flaws, strengths, self-defeating behaviours, victories, joys and sorrows. That includes you and your love-partner. This fact makes it easier to talk about our weaknesses and easier not to judge others for theirs.

The answer, again, is for the talker to find the courage to talk and for the listener to make it safe. This is done with non-judgmental acceptance, understanding, and love. Having your love-partner know and accept your weaknesses is a powerful balm. It helps you feel worthwhile. It also gives your partner permission to have their own weaknesses and to share them with you.

THM: Listening to and accepting weaknesses is a powerful balm.

When you listen to someone talk about their weaknesses, be very gentle. Listen lovingly. They need to know that you will not reject or abandon them. They are likely feeling shameful. Be gentle with this. They are privileging you with great trust.

THM: Be gentle; very, very gentle.

Listening to dreams and ideas

Sometimes we have wild, exciting ideas: moving to a new country, changing jobs, changing lifestyle, or pursuing an interest passionately. But it may sound too far-fetched, too different or involve too much effort, so the ideas often do not get shared. We think they may cause conflict and be rejected as silly or too idealistic, so we silently keep the peace.

To avoid conflict with a loving-partner, many people share their criticisms, details of sexual intimacy, their own weaknesses, or dreams and ideas with friends or drinking mates. With these people, there is little risk of rejection; there is very little at stake. You are privileging them with information, but this can come at the cost of alienating your love-partner.

The situation can be overcome by good listening. With good listening, your love-partner can trust you to be their best friend and confidante. Listening to future dreams does not necessarily mean they'll happen. Just listen, dream along, and consider the *what ifs* of this future together. Try to shelve your practical opinions for a while and just listen. Dream with them. If conflicts emerge, just accept the conflict. Let it be. You are looking at the truth of someone's dreams. This is better than them bottling up dreams or ideas. Who knows, maybe a part of the dream could come true?

Listen. Let them soar in their minds. Soar with them if you can. Explore. Enjoy the dream, and the intimacy of sharing it (before going on to problem-solving and harsh realities).

THM: Listen to dreams and ideas. Soar together before considering reality.

You, the listener, will have to be vigilant in shelving your own beliefs, judgments and needs for a while. After the listening session, don't come out with guns blazing: *right, now you're going to listen to <u>my</u> dreams and ideas!* Wait. Let it sit for a while. Give it time. Give your loving-partner the message of *yes, I have heard and accepted your ideas.* You will soon get your turn.

Every now and again, a couple will face the pain of having to face up to something extremely difficult; something which could jeopardize the whole relationship. In these cases, it is best to consider looking to professionals to handle your particular situation. Ask for help if you need it.

Through good listening, difficult issues in a relationship can be safely shared; particularly in the most important relationship in your life. It is worth trying to get it right with your love-partner. It is worth the time and effort to listen. Listening helps reach the deep intimacy that comes with fuller acceptance, understanding and expression of each other.

Summary

It's easy to understand that the more thoughts and feelings you can share with one another, the closer you will be as a couple. Listening facilitates this.

Communication in a love relationship is unique: you are special to one another, you are with each other for so much of the time, you want peace and harmony yet you have wants and needs to honestly express. This naturally leads to conflict: arguments or the silent treatment.

Navigating thorny issues with active listening engenders trust and acceptance. Even difficult issues – sharing what seems like criticism, discussing sexual intimacy, personal weaknesses and future dreams – can be safely expressed. A relationship is like a complex piece of music: it has times of dissonance and drama but also times of tranquillity and repose.

The aim is harmony.

Some people only hear their love-partner as though they are nothing more than another sound around them. Others listen briefly and occasionally notice the meaning and emotion underneath the words. You can listen actively to your love-partner, to accept and trust them, to be there fully with them, and to uncover and share more wonderful moments of emotional intimacy.

After all, listening is a way of saying *I love you.*

Remember to extrapolate the lessons and techniques you use in listening to your love-partner to listen to other people in other situations.

CHAPTER FOUR

The Science of Listening

So, the first three chapters were too touchy-feely, huh? I hear you. I'm listening. This chapter should even up the score. I'll be scientific here: technical, informative. I'll talk facts instead of concepts. (Well, as much as I can.)

The brain is where we experience life. The brain is where we talk and listen. The brain is where the ingredients of active listening come together: attention and focus, recognition of non-verbal communication, empathy and compassion in the anterior cingulate gyrus, mirror neurons, trust and oxytocin, logic in the left brain, and belief in the right brain.

Understanding these things will help you in your active listening. Throughout this chapter, I'll apply the knowledge directly to listening. Getting to know what your brain does in listening is a bit like looking under the hood of your car, or knowing how the human genitalia work: understanding enhances the experience. It's also interesting.

At the very least, this chapter will give you the confidence to know that what I'm saying in this book is based on science and some anatomical structures which reside in the space between your ears.

In fact, let's start with the ears.

The hearing pathway

This is a brief, fun overview of how we hear. The ears magically convert vibration into electronic nerve signals, and these register in the brain for us to experience.

Sound hits the outer ear and bounces around like a funnel. It whacks the ear drum, and travels through the three states of matter: air, solid bone, and liquid in the middle ear. In the inner ear, the sound becomes nerve signals, thanks to vibrating liquid moving thousands of tiny little hairs. (Bats have many more of these tiny little hair cells in their ears.) The signals then move into the brain via the auditory nerve, a bit like electricity in a wire.

The nerve signals enter the room of the brain's gate-keeper: the thalamus. "Thalamus" just means room. It sits on the brainstem like a koala holding a tree trunk. Its job it to decide which signals reach the brain's awareness (the thalamus's job, not the koala's). If it's important, the thalamus will make the brain aware of it. If it's unimportant – like the sound of someone calling you for dinner while you're on the computer – it probably won't register. Here's where listening comes in. Our brain awareness can say to the thalamus *hey, give me more of those sounds I'm interested in, but less dinner calls. Thanks!*

The sound then reaches the brain's awareness at the auditory cortex at the left posterior superior temporal gyrus (that's the hearing part at the upper fat bulgy-bit on the arse-end of the left side of the outside crust of the brain). Simple, right? This bit of the brain has connections with the thinking, feeling and movement bits of the brain. We then think, feel, and decide whether to do something because of the sound. (Don't take too long if it's a cracking tree branch.)

You don't really need to know any of that. It's just interesting. More important to listening is your focus, attention and concentration.

Focus, attention and concentration

Active listening requires focus, attention and concentration. <u>Attention</u> is that magical quality of consciousness which lets us know we are alive: *I think, therefore I know I am*. We can <u>focus</u> our attention wherever we decide to. It's like a flashlight: we can have a broad or narrow focus, with varying amounts of intensity, and we decide where to focus it. When we <u>concentrate</u>, we focus our attention sharply and narrowly to a small central point, idea or task. When we are not concentrating, our attention is less focussed and we are more distractible.

We can only focus our attention on one thing at a time.[4] (People who believe they can multi-task are actually in a state of perpetual, partial inattention.) If, for example, you do something else while driving, like texting, you are putting yourself and others at grave risk.[5] That's why it's illegal (or should be). If you do something else while listening – like reading a paper or watching a computer screen – you are not really listening, you are partially listening and partially reading. The talker feels that our listening efforts are only half-hearted.

THM: We can only focus on one thing at a time. When listening, only listen.

With more focus, attention and concentration, hearing moves through listening to active listening.

In the brain, we have two attention systems: a primitive, automatic one to keep us alive, and a sophisticated one which we can control. The one that keeps you alive is like an alarm system. It makes sure you don't take too long to react if you hear a tree-branch snap. It's primitive because lower life forms like crocodiles have this system too. Scientists call it the "bottom-up" system (because what comes from your bottom is primitive). It's part of your reticular activating system.

Your reticular activating system (RAS) plays an important role in keeping you alert and aroused; it lives in your brainstem. (Crocodiles have brainstems too so they have a RAS.) It directs your attention to danger: snakes, sharks and falling tree-branches. In a soldier, for example, the RAS alerts the brain to look for clues of the enemy: colour, shape and movement. It is important for survival.

Your RAS responds to things on your mind. Whenever you've bought a new car, for instance, you suddenly notice how many cars like your new one are on the road. That's your RAS alarming you to look at something you are interested in. My training as a doctor keeps my RAS on the lookout on how to avoid infections: a cough or sneeze by someone near me alarms me. My love-partner has a RAS keenly trained to look out for sales and bargains. Her RAS can quickly find bargains and sales, even in foreign languages.

With practice in listening, your RAS alerts you about important cues coming from the talker: nostril flares and eye twitches, for example. These could be signs of danger. It can also alert you to changes in tone, pitch and the significance of sudden silence, once you are well enough trained.

Our more sophisticated attention system is in our frontal lobe. (Crocodiles and other flat-headed creatures barely have a frontal lobe so they don't have this sophisticated system; they are bad listeners.) But we have to <u>decide</u> to use this system, and that means voluntary effort. We are capable of focussing our attention to anything we believe is relevant.[6] Our primitive alarm system almost shouts out to our awareness *Crap!! Move! Falling branch!!* Our more sophisticated attention system – the one we can control and have to decide to use – kicks in later (if we want it to) to bring our attention to a fallen branch and ask *why did that tree-branch break just then?*

Using the flashlight analogy, we can appreciate that in general hearing, our attention is weak but broad. In listening it becomes stronger and narrower – focussed on a single sound perhaps. In active listening, as we concentrate, it becomes even stronger and narrower – focussed even on a part of a sound. This takes energy and is not automatic.

THM: *In active listening, concentrate.*

We <u>hear</u> people's voices around us without giving them too much attention. We can focus our attention flashlight on what one person is saying if we are interested. This is <u>listening</u>. We can focus it narrower on what they say about one subject and how they feel about it. This takes concentration and energy. Distracting text messages and demanding cats become less important for a short while. This is <u>active listening</u>: more attention, focus and concentration.

Non-verbal communication

In listening, we don't just focus our attention on words. Our attention also picks up information from the tone, volume, speed and pitch of someone's voice. It also picks up a lot from non-verbal communication.

Non-verbal communication is the expression of emotions and information through anything but words. (You already knew that.) If someone hits you or hugs you, they have expressed a lot without using words. This is a form of non-verbal communication. Other forms of non-verbal communication include hand gestures, body movements, penetration of gaze, facial expressions, voice quality, posture, clothing and more.

Charles Darwin noticed the universality of expressions in man and animals and wrote a whole book on this. He saw the connection between emotions and body movements, particularly facial expressions. The word emotion means "moving out," so the connection between emotions and movement is natural. He saw that *expression is to [emotion] as language is to thought*[7] and concluded that *the force of language is much aided by the expressive movements of the face and body.*[8] He was describing non-verbals.

Through reading people's facial expressions and their body movements, we understand more about the emotions underneath their words. In listening, we listen to someone's emotions through non-verbal communication as much as through their words.

In 1952, anthropologist Ray Birdwhistell published his initial studies on body language.[9] This has developed into a whole field of knowledge. Posture, for example, can be open (arms and legs unfolded and relaxed indicating a willingness to receive information) or closed (arms and legs folded indicating a more sceptical *convince me* attitude). Clothing is non-verbal expression; it can be provocative, conservative, seductive or conformist. Hand gestures and hand-shakes can express confidence, flamboyance, modesty or anger; and gaze can suggest sexual allure, compassion, indifference or disdain.

Non-verbals may reveal information not heard in a person's words. They may not. They impart information, but this form of information is vague and open to misinterpretation. Words are precise, but people may lie or mislead. Combine the two: does a person's expressions and body language match their words? Why or why not? Do their words tell me one thing but their facial expression another? Non-verbals are important in listening but don't place too much emphasis on them either.

THM: When listening, compare a person's words with their non-verbals.

Be aware of what messages or signals you the listener give to the talker through your non-verbals. As a general rule, try to keep an open posture by keeping your arms and legs uncrossed. This shows you are open to their ideas. Keep your expression neutral and warm, use touch if that is appropriate to your listening situation. Don't let your eyes wander over the room, and don't use a harsh, abrasive, loud voice. Speak softly, keep attention fixed on the talker, and try to "match" their energy levels, volume and pace.

THM: Be aware of the signals you are giving through non-verbals.

If, as the listener, you use non-threatening facial expressions and body posture, you help "make it safe" for the talker. You communicate the idea that *I'm just like you.* Humans are, on the whole, social creatures looking for social cohesion and security. To further a sense of safety, trust and acceptance, we can use our keen sense of empathy and compassion.

Empathy and compassion: the anterior cingulate gyrus

Empathy is the capacity to share in the feelings of another person. Compassion is concern for another person's suffering. Empathy and compassion, along with bonding, identifying, sympathizing, admiring, caring and sharing, (and all that kind of stuff) are highly evolved in humans to aid in our social cohesion. Without these capacities, we probably could not have survived.

A human baby, for example, cannot survive alone, it needs to be taken care of for a very long time in comparison with other species. It needs to bond to a parent and be cared for. That parent needs to have empathy and compassion to do this. Often, parents tell me that *having a child is like living with your heart outside your body*. I am a parent. I know exactly what that means. Even though my children are adults, I still feel their pain, worry about them, and share in their triumphs. That's empathy and compassion.

We do this to some extent with every fellow human being. Children are very close, so the feelings are very strong. With family members and friends, the feelings are still strong. With people who share nationality, some kinship is still there, but the feelings become less strong. Although we share something important with these people, we identify with them less.

Feelings of socialization are experienced in the anterior cingulate gyrus (ACG), deep inside the brain, under the cortex, next to the prefrontal cortex and the limbic system. It connects with our thinking (in the prefrontal cortex) and feelings (in the limbic system). "Gut feelings" emanate from this region. The ACG allows us to be aware of and to regulate our own emotions in the presence of others. This is also what listening does. It harmonizes our thoughts and feelings with the thoughts and feelings of another person.

The ACG is very active in empathic and compassionate listeners. Your anterior cingulate gyrus will become more active and develop as you practice listening. *Can I really develop different parts of my brain just by listening?* Yes, you can.[10]

Having empathy and compassion helps greatly in active listening. These are the qualities we must have in abundance so the talker can feel heard, understood and valued. They are the brain tools that reach to the ultimate goal in active listening: being there in a trusting relationship with another human being.

THM: *Empathy and compassion help us to connect.*

Empathy and compassion allow you to resonate with the soft flute of a friend's need underneath the crashing cymbals of day-to-day life.

Mirror neurons

In the early 1990s, a team of scientists in Italy made a remarkable discovery. Through implanted electrodes, they found that one monkey's brain "fired" while it was watching another monkey reach for a banana. The "firing" showed that the watching monkey <u>knew</u> that the other monkey wanted to eat the banana. The watching monkey understood the <u>intention</u> of the other monkey. This seemed like mental telepathy between monkeys. It demanded an explanation. The theory of mirror neurons was born.

According to this theory, mammals have specialized brain cells which, through the eyes, can read other's intentions. These neurons "mirror" what is happening in another brain. There may be literal truth in the saying *the eyes are the mirror of the soul.*

Mirror neurons have been linked to understanding goals and intentions, empathy, imitation, monitoring others' emotions, understanding and reading social cues, and chiming in with a new culture. Mirror neurons may be the mechanism linking one person's ACG with another. (Perhaps autism results from a deficit in mirror neuron function.)

If mirror neurons mediate the flow of empathy and compassion among humans, then they are important in listening. It is no wonder that looking someone in the eye can say so much. But it would be strange that this system worked through eyes only. Blind people are empathic and compassionate and are sensitive to sounds and the nuances of feelings. I believe that mirror neurons are activated by hearing, touch and other senses. Just think of how much intention, empathy and emotion monitoring is communicated by a hug.

Mirror neuron research is ongoing. Most of the research involves eye contact because that's where the evidence is. When you are listening, it is eye contact which most transmits that feeling of empathy and compassion. These feelings, I believe, can also be transmitted through the warmth of the voice, or through physical touch. Together, these allow the talker to feel heard, understood and accepted.

THM: Eye contact is important; eyes are the mirror of the soul.

Trust and oxytocin

Let's get chemical. Let's talk trust. The chemical is oxytocin and it's my favourite brain chemical. (I know, a psychiatrist isn't supposed to have favourite brain chemicals, but I do.) It mediates the love and care we feel in hugs, smiles, kisses, sex, and listening. It can be measured scientifically. It mediates feelings of trust and good will among people. Caring, love, socializing and trust are connected in the brain via oxytocin.

Good listening engenders trust, so it increases oxytocin levels. Scientists have been able to measure oxytocin levels in mothers in a birthing suite, in couples getting married, and in people who trust each other in relationships and in business transactions.[11] When one person is really listening to another, oxytocin mediates trust and caring feelings. Oxytocin feels very good; it is the hug-drug. This is why active listening is a way of saying *I love you, I care for you.* Trust and oxytocin help make each listening session a unique experience. They make a person feel they are not alone.

THM: *Through oxytocin, listening makes another person feel cared for.*

Current scientific evidence suggests that empathy, compassion, caring, trust and socialization are mediated in the anterior cingulate gyrus anatomically; through mirror neurons which fire electrically; and through oxytocin chemically. These are not separate systems, they are part of a complex, integrated whole that we do not fully understand: the brain.

The left and right brains

Just before we leave the brain and the science of listening, I want us to consider how difficult it is to suspend judgment and shelve beliefs. There is a good reason for this, and it lies in how our left and right brains work.

The brain is actually two separate brains, one on the left and one on the right. They are joined by a huge bundle of nerves called the corpus callosum, "the big body" of nerves. If you cut through this big bundle of nerves, the left and the right brains would work independently, but they couldn't talk to each other or coordinate.

The thinking bits of the brains are at the front: the frontal lobes. The left frontal lobe basically takes care of logic, calculations and words; the things that are common to all people around us. The right frontal lobe takes care of beliefs and opinions; the things that make us unique individuals. When there is an apparent conflict between logic and our beliefs, right brain belief wins out.[12] For all of us.

Let's take a few examples to illustrate this curiosity.

In 2005, the BBC reported that an injured woman lifted twenty times her body weight to save a man who was trapped underneath a car.[13] In 1917, in Portugal, the mother of Christ appeared to a child and, in front of 70,000 people, made the sun dance around in the sky.[14]

Do miracles occur or not?

The answer <u>you</u> come up with will depend on your right-brain belief. Some theists, persons of faith, may conclude that miracles are real. A sceptic concludes that a logical explanation is yet to be found. A psychological explanation <u>has</u> been offered for the sun dance, but science still cannot explain the car lift. Even if an explanation is found, it may or may not reflect the truth of the situation; it may just be an explanation. We don't know. Left brain logic is not enough.

For both the believer and the sceptic, there is a dilemma when logic cannot explain what happened. They may agree on certain facts, but when we reach the limit of available facts, right-brain thinking kicks in (for all of us). We all form opinions in such cases based on our individual beliefs. This is the case in politics, social conventions, ethical dilemmas and whether it is abusive or not to teach children about Santa Claus. It is difficult for anyone – the believer and sceptic included – to just "leave it hanging," "leave it up in the air," or "let it sit."

THM: Belief tends to trump logic in the brain.

We form beliefs and opinions because that's how the brain works. Some people may wish we were all left-brain, logical, and always able to agree with each other, but it's the right brain which makes us individuals. All our differing tastes, cultures, arts, idiosyncrasies, likes and dislikes are thanks to right brain beliefs. The world would be pretty bland without it.

So, as a listener, it takes conscious voluntary effort <u>not</u> to make a judgment. You need to say *OK, this person believes something I don't. I know me, but I'll just allow them to say what they say, believe what they believe, and let them be, so I can understand* <u>*them*</u>*. I'll try to understand and accept how* <u>*their*</u> *world works for them.* This is strangely difficult to do. It's like our brain has a constant need to say *yes, but this is* <u>*me*</u>*! This is how I think! This is who I am!*

It is a skill to just leave it hanging, leave it up in the air, or let it sit. But this is what we need to do while we listen, particularly to someone with opposing beliefs and opinions. This takes practice. People who prefer the left or the right side of politics, or who believe or not in an afterlife, or who believe in conspiracy theories or not, aren't idiots or morons, they have different beliefs.

THM: *Beliefs and opinions make us different.*

When we practice the skill of shelving our beliefs, a talker can feel accepted as a fully thinking, fully feeling, equal individual person. And that can make all the difference.

Summary

Understanding how hearing, focus, attention and concentration, non-verbals, mirror neurons, oxytocin, and empathy and compassion work in the brain, helps us in active listening. These elements exist in the brain, one of our last frontiers of exploration. Active listening is not some vague, ill-defined mythical magic, it is steeped in scientific knowledge we all have access to.

We all have a brain. We are all capable of active listening. And we could all benefit from having more of it in our lives.

CHAPTER FIVE

Deeper listening

Brace yourself. In this final chapter, we go the whole hog, pull out all stops, and go full-throttle for deeper listening: for information, for feelings, and just to be there for a fellow human being. First, however, we discuss Carl Roger's notion of unconditional positive regard. This is a very important beginning to going deeper in listening.

Unconditional positive regard

You can figure out what unconditional positive regard is: seeing the other person in a positive light no matter what. It is total acceptance of who they are. Unconditional positive regard is a core concept in the work of Carl Rogers, a humanist psychologist. It is "prizing," valuing and accepting a person, no matter what.[15] According to Rogers, if we can truly accept someone, they can accept themselves, and tap into their own resources for healing.

You already have something more than positive regard for your partner, parent, child or friends. Love. To have <u>unconditional</u> love is a very high ideal. Unconditional positive regard doesn't quite reach that high. It is easier. It is a skill. You develop it by doing the listening basics.

Now I have to contradict Rogers. It's not really possible to have unconditional positive regard. It's always conditional. If a person starts hitting me, I tend to lose my positive regard for them. I have my limits, and everyone does. The trick is to have as much unconditional positive regard as you can; to get away from the I'll-only-accept-you-if-you-agree-with-me syndrome so prevalent in human interactions. Allowing the other person to be who they are, and accepting them, is part of the gift of listening.

Practical tips for developing unconditional positive regard

1. <u>Suspend judgment</u>. Shelve your beliefs and opinions. One of our greatest fears as humans is being judged. We are social creatures; being judged is the first step to being ousted, ostracized, or banished. Nobody wants that. A talker may be judging themselves harshly enough anyway. The last thing they need is some other shmuck pouring salt over their wounds.

Suspending judgment takes a little self-pep-talk to remind yourself to do it. It's difficult to do because of the left-brain/right-brain dilemma. Suspending judgment also takes putting into practice what you learnt in listening to nature, music or the theatre. You don't judge nature sounds; you just let them be. You may dislike the play but you don't change the script; you let it be. You may dislike the music, but the most you can do is walk away. Don't walk away from a person. A person has feelings. Let them be who they are.

THM: A person has feelings; don't walk away.

2. <u>Don't problem-solve</u>. Problem-solving shows you haven't accepted the person just as they are. It shows you are uncomfortable with their situation and therefore uncomfortable with them; that's not accepting them. Refrain from problem-solving to show unconditional positive regard.

3. <u>Value what they say</u>. Thank them occasionally:

> *Thank you for sharing that.*
> *That was hard to hear but thanks.*
> *Thanks for caring enough to tell me that.*
> *I understand, thank you.*

Thanking is like giving a gift. It's the "prizing" part of unconditional positive regard.

4. <u>Make eye contact</u>. This shows that you are interested in the talker as a person. Remember the mirror neurons. Eye contact transmits empathy and compassion and shows that you care. It shows you have unconditional positive regard.

5. <u>Find something you like about the talker</u>. The talker's fear is that you may not like or accept them. In listening to your love-partner, for example, there are usually many things you like about them. Just now, however, when they need you to listen about how you turn up late, or about a plan you may not approve of, it's funny how all those things you like about them quickly

fade away. All of a sudden you can only think of what you've had to put up with all these years.

Think about how beautiful they are; how they know you so well; how they know how to comfort you; how loving they are to your children; how thoughtful they can be. Any thoughts you have about how you like or love them will shine through your eyes, into their mirror neurons, into their ACG, and they will feel accepted.

If you are listening to one of your least favourite relatives it becomes more important to find something you like. Everybody has strengths, but because of ill feelings, you don't really want to think about them at the moment. Find them. Think of them.

If you are listening to someone you <u>really</u> don't like, find something immediate to like:

> *I like their hair.*
> *I've never noticed how pleasing their voice is.*
> *I admire how much guts they have to talk to me about this.*
> *I know this person is a good father.*

Find something to like about the talker and think about it. This will help foster unconditional positive regard.

6. <u>Be yourself</u>. This sounds like a strange thing to do to help the other person feel accepted, but it helps. If you are OK about you being yourself, then, through mirror neurons, they can feel OK

about being themselves. Just don't arrogantly feel superior to them; this will alienate them. Ultimately, you are both human beings trying to get through this crazy thing called life. We all equalize on that.

If, however, a talker does not feel comfortable about being themselves no matter what you do, that's OK too. This too cries out for acceptance. Accept it; don't try to fix it. Let it be.

THM: Cultivate unconditional positive regard.

If you can do these things – and they are not easy – you will be listening deeper, with more unconditional positive regard.

Listening for information

Listening for information is particularly needed in work situations. It is also important in all relationship listening. If you listen to someone well, you will 'get' more of their information; even things they can't put into words.

To listen deeper for information, slow down, take time, and make a connection. Ask about feelings as well as information. Knowing about their feelings gives you important information. Build trust and do the six listening basics. All this gets the oxytocin pumping; it even makes for better business relationships.[16]

I listen for information all of the time. I am trained to do this. In psychotherapy, however, listening for information takes on an added dimension. Through listening for information, I build rapport and trust. The listening process itself becomes healing; therapeutic.

One of the first things I do is take a history. This may take anywhere from one to five sessions. The best way to describe what really goes on, and how it is relevant to listening, is that I try not to <u>take</u> a history, I try to <u>receive</u> a history. The difference? When I <u>take</u> a history, it's all about me and my agenda to be able to treat the person. When I <u>receive</u> a history, it's all about the other person, their agenda, and what they need to let me know. I still need to get the information I need to work with that person, but my primary aim is to be there and to actively listen with unconditional positive regard.

In listening for information, clarifying questions become important:

> *And then what happened?*
> *Can you tell me more about that?*
> *I think I understand. You were … is that right?*
> *Who? What? Where? When? How? Which?*

Why is missing from the questions list. *Why* is often too direct, too confrontational, and too anxiety-provoking. Some alternatives include:

How come?
What was your purpose in doing that?
Was there a particular reason you did that?
And you did that because … (invitation to speak).

Avoiding *why*, however, can get artificial with people close to you. They may feel that you are handling them with kid gloves. They know you. Be real.

Don't sound like a detective when asking questions. Already better is to think of yourself as a talk-show host who likes to listen; (not all do).

Questions need to be asked with interest. The purpose of questions is to enhance your understanding of the situation for <u>their</u> benefit, not yours.

Just to clarify this for me, you said that … but … so … is that what you meant?
I need to know about … . You said … but I don't know … .
Could you help me out?
Is there anything else you need me to know?

Some questions will ask for opinions rather than facts.

What do <u>you</u> believe about this situation?
What do you tell yourself is happening?
Do you feel OK about this deal / our agreement?

Listening for information is something you can do in all situations: at work, with friends, family or with your love-partner. This type of listening is usually followed by problem-solving. Don't let it become dry and routine. You are listening to a full-blooded, living, thinking, feeling person. Be there; sharing this part of their life with them.

Even in business transactions it is appropriate to ask about feelings. By asking about someone's feelings, you are gaining vital information. Try replacing the usual so *what do you think about that?* with *so how do you feel about that?* Monitor your results with this.

THM: Asking about feelings gives you information.

These techniques will help you go deeper in your listening for information. You'll be surprised how good the results will be, particularly in your relationship with the person giving you the information. You will also remember any information given to you much better.

Listening for feelings

In every listening interaction, we listen for information. We are obsessed with information. We live in a society which is focussed on information, data, and knowledge. We think that more information helps. In this information focus, we naturally become problem-solvers because we believe that is the only way to go forward in life. We look at the logical side of any equation and often pay little attention to feelings.

From childhood on, we are trained to be logical, reasonable and rational.

Fine. There's nothing wrong with being logical, reasonable and rational. It is logic which gives us an intellectual edge over other creatures. We are, however, still social creatures and feeling creatures as well as thinking creatures. Often our feelings are often neglected to our detriment.

Listening for feelings can balance things up.

Most of us can reason out our logic-based day-to-day problems on our own. But, at some time or another, we feel alone, misunderstood, unheard, hurt, and alienated. We may feel that we cannot move forward. This is not a problem of logic, we become overwhelmed by feelings.

At these times, it is beneficial to have someone simply listen. Not just listen <u>to</u> our feelings but also listen <u>for</u> our feelings. Listening <u>to</u> feelings means listening to someone articulate their feelings through words. Listening <u>for</u> feelings is actively sensing and being sensitive to a person's feelings apart from their words and in their non-verbals: tone of voice, volume, behaviours, gestures, and facial expressions.

It's like listening to a piece of music. Listening to music is almost a magical experience. We get moved by music and feel things through music without understanding how or why. We enjoy it. It evokes feelings in us. We listen <u>for</u> the feelings in music. Feelings and meanings in music are conveyed through the rhythm, melody, harmonies, sound-colours, and the role of specific instruments. You can pick up more feeling and meanings in music when you listen to these elements as closely as you can. That's what I encouraged you to do in Chapter Two.

Another person is much more intricate than any piece of music. Listen for their feelings in them any way you can. The best way I can describe to you how to do this, is articulate what happens when you listen to music: you leave yourself "open" to the music; you give yourself to it; you let it take you and affect you. Then when a piece of music comes on that you don't like, you will notice that you "close" yourself off to it; you stop listening until the music changes back to something you like.

So, the aim is to keep yourself "open" to the person you are listening to: accept them, like them, receive them, and let their thoughts and feelings affect and impact your thoughts and feelings. You will notice if you "close" yourself off from anybody. This usually happens because you do not like them or they say something you do not believe. When this happens during listening, you will need to use techniques – the six listening basics and those for developing unconditional positive regard – to keep yourself "open" to them.

This way, you will be listening for feelings, and you will drink those feelings into your sponge self as you listen.

THM: Keep yourself "open" to a person as you do to music you like.

Listening for feelings is rewarding and helps us understand and accept any person. Listening for feelings, however, can be imprecise and vague. Mistakes can be made. Feelings can be misinterpreted, misunderstood and missed. We may think someone is cheerful when they are irritated; we may think they are nervous when they are excited; we may think they are disappointed in us when actually they are having trouble expressing just how proud they are of us.

The ambiguity and inherent complexities of feelings-based communication makes us uncomfortable. We don't want to get it wrong, so we avoid it. In the context of listening to someone, however, don't avoid it, just don't jump to conclusions about what they may or may not be feeling. When you have picked up on a feeling, just file it away. This takes practice.

THM: Don't jump to conclusions about feelings.

The benefits of listening for feelings greatly outweighs any problems. Most people do not get enough opportunity to express their feelings or have their feelings accepted and understood. Any efforts made in this area will be helpful and healing.

To listen for feelings, ask questions about feelings:

> *How do you feel about that?*
> *What did you feel just then?*
> *Did that sadden you?*

By naming a feeling you believe the talker is experiencing, it shows that you are comfortable with talking about feelings.

Also "listen" to their non-verbal communications. Listening for non-verbals entails noticing, watching and monitoring your "gut feelings" about something you notice.

> Are their feet jittering out of anxiety?
> Are they crying out of sadness or joy?
> Are they motionless out of dejection or shame?
> Is their face screwed up out of frustration?
> Are they silent out of anger, embarrassment or fear?
> Is their gaze penetrating out of hate or expectation?

Listen. Listen to the non-verbals. Listen for the feelings.

You may notice something in their demeanour or body language; you may ask if they feel a certain emotion. It is always good to bring cool reason to hot emotions. This process begins by naming the emotion. Once we have a word for the emotion, we capture it and look at it. It doesn't capture us. This is good.

It is useful to have a little lexicon of emotions to articulate them with precision. Words help understanding and communication.

A lexicon of emotions

Many people are already comfortable with dealing with and expressing emotions. If you're one of them, you can skip this section. Other people are more thinking-based. That's OK. To get you comfortable with naming emotions, and working with them, here's a logical approach to categorizing them.

There are many classification systems for emotions. I'll simplify the one by Robert Plutchik.[17] He articulated four pairs of basic emotions:

> 1. Joy and sadness (opposites as joy is uplifting, sadness is downtrodden)
> 2. Trust and disgust (opposites as trust draws you in, disgust repels you)
> 3. Anger and fear (opposites as anger intrudes forward, fear withdraws back)
> 4. Surprise and anticipation (opposites as surprise has experienced, anticipation hasn't)

Two are paired positives and negatives: joy and sadness, trust and disgust; anger and fear are both negative but anger moves towards and fear moves back; surprise and anticipation are both positive but surprise comes after an event, anticipation before.

Let's look at the four positive emotions: joy, trust, surprise and anticipation. They can occur in a mild form, a moderate form and a severe form.

Mild	_Moderate_	_Severe_
Serenity	**joy**	ecstasy
Acceptance	**trust**	admiration
Distraction	**surprise**	amazement
Interest	**anticipation**	vigilance

Now let's look at the negative emotions. I will concentrate on the negative emotions here as those are the ones we need to be aware of in times of crises. For your own interest, however, look at the positive ones as well. Moving from mild – moderate – severe in the negative emotions we see the following:

Mild	_Moderate_	_Severe_
Pensiveness	**sadness**	grief
Boredom	**disgust**	loathing
Annoyance	**anger**	rage
Apprehension	**fear**	terror

We can understand what sadness is: a down, unhappy state. Pensiveness, and related emotions such as reflection, despondency, and gloom, are "mild sadness;" and grief, and related emotions such as depression, desolation, and despair, are "severe sadness." Also relevant are feelings such as melancholy, sorrow, and mournfulness.

Disgust is a visceral feeling of revulsion towards something offensive. Boredom, and dislike and distaste, are "mild disgust;" and loathing, and hatred and revulsion, are "severe disgust." Relevant too are shame (disgust at oneself), embarrassment (shame caused by and felt in the presence of others), mortification, humiliation and disgrace.

Anger is a visceral feeling of hostility towards something or someone, often caused by an actual or perceived injustice. Annoyance, and irritation and frustration, are "mild anger;" and rage, and infuriation and outrage, are "severe anger." Other emotions relevant to anger include resentment (more intellectual than anger), bitterness (colder and less aggressive than anger), exasperation, and indignation.

Fear is a visceral feeling of foreboding caused by a real threat. Apprehension, and dismay and trepidation, are "mild fear;" and terror, and horror and panic, are "severe fear." Anxiety is caused by an imagined threat. Other relevant emotions in this area include concern, worry, alarm, suspicion, uneasiness, disquiet and dread.

Other negative emotions to be aware of include contempt, remorse, disapproval, envy, lust, jealousy, bewilderment, and shock. There are many other positive emotions including hope, delight, curiosity, optimism, awe and love. The categorizing and understanding of emotions is a study in itself. You can go further in this with a dictionary and thesaurus on the internet.

THM: Build your own lexicon of emotions.

Using words to name emotions is using thoughts to understand feelings. Feelings can be elusive. Sometimes they can only be articulated and understood days after experiencing them. Having someone close-by to listen to our feelings so that we are not alone with them is extremely helpful.

Listening for feelings is a healing balm for the talker. Being accepted, and having someone share this part of life means that there is less chance in being overwhelmed by emotions.

Just being there

It's time to give you the real secret of active listening. The final disclosure. Why is listening so important and such a gift to another person? Because we are social creatures. None of us wants to be alone. Listening is deep acceptance; it is just being there for another person as a fellow human being. That's the gift. That's the real point.

None of us want to be alone; particularly not in a crisis.

Just being there means you can help hold the emotions for someone else. They will be less likely to be overwhelmed by their emotions. They will not be alone. You will, in a very real sense, become a container, a vessel, into which they can pour their emotions. This extends the sponge analogy.

THM: Listening is containing emotions for someone else.

When I trained with the ambulance service, we never left an accident victim alone. The mere presence of another human being was vital. It was not only comforting, it was life-saving. An accident victim is in a desperate state. Their life may be threatened and they are experiencing an overwhelming array of emotions. They may not wish to share these emotions or may not be able to, but it is always helpful to have someone there to help contain the emotional load. Nobody wants to be alone, particularly in a crisis.

THM: *Nobody wants to be alone.*

We need each other. We need to be in the presence of other people. That's why solitary confinement is such harsh punishment. It is difficult for most of us to appreciate this, because we always have access to other people.

When someone is in a crisis, they want access to other people.

We are usually together with people to the point that, for some of us, others can get annoying. We even feel the need to get away from them. In listening, however, we take time and space away from our busyness, noise and social masks to allow someone to be themselves in our presence; to just be there. This is not annoying. This is real. They can take off their social mask as we take off ours, at least a little. We make ourselves vulnerable to share in their vulnerability.

THM: *Listening is shared vulnerability.*

Just being there for the other person is the easiest type of listening, and the hardest type of listening. Sometimes I have sessions with the people I treat, when I say and do almost nothing. Sometimes they just cry … for the best part of an hour. All I do is just be there. But I am there with intent, fully with them during this time.

What makes this type of listening difficult is resisting the urge to say something; to make conversation. Perhaps the most I may say is *it's OK*. The idea is simply to be there. To wait. Patiently. To allow them to cut the silence if <u>they</u> want to.

Just being there for someone creates an atmosphere where the other person feels free to be themselves. Really free to be themselves. It's OK. You give them permission to be themselves, however that may be, even if they may not be allowing this. In their minds they may be chastising themselves for being weak, for hurting, or taking up someone else's time. By being there, you can help free someone from their own chains.

Let's take a closer look at the ambulance situation with the accident victim.

It seems obvious, but the person does not want to be in that situation in the first place. It's lonely. They do not want to be hurting and needing help. They often feel that they are a burden. They are in need of help; fearful that their life could end; losing hope. Hope is important. As a listener, you preserve hope for them.

THM: *Listening preserves hope.*

What do you do in a crisis situation and you are not a trained professional? Beyond basic safety and resuscitation techniques, just be there. Do not leave them alone. You don't have to do anything else. You may answer a few questions; you may share in any small talk or silly, private humour they may offer. Your biggest job is to try not to feel you have to say something. Just be there.

THM: *Just be there.*

It's the same with your love-partner, a relative, a friend, a colleague or a stranger. They may not be in a life-threatening crisis, but every emotional upheaval – no matter how small – is a mini-crisis. It threatens some part of their life. It may threaten who they are, their security, their reputation, or their sense of self. They may be in a flood of tears. They may be angry. You could ask *is there anything you want me to do?* Beyond that, sometimes you only need to be there.

If, in their anger or embarrassment they say to you *just leave me alone!* Ask if they really want you to leave. If it is, you will need to make a judgment call based on what you know is best for them in this situation. (Remember, in their hurt, they may still not want you to leave, in spite of their words.) If you feel they really want you to leave, at the very least leave with a door open: *I'll be back whenever you need me, just call … I'll stop by tomorrow if you like.* Never leave anyone if it may be dangerous to do so. Safety first. Always.

THM: Even in listening, remember safety first.

While you are with someone in a crisis, just let time pass. Don't fuss. Say nothing and do nothing. Just be there. Make sure they know you are there, with an occasional touch, an occasional glance, sometimes an encouraging word. Listen to anything they may say, but listen more to their tears or listen to their silence. This can be very powerful.

What's happening? In just being there, you are making sure they are not alone. You are creating a shared moment. You are journeying with them. The alternative is them forever remembering that they had to go through a difficult moment alone. Not good.

Having shared this little part of their journey, these moments become part of your life's journey as well. It becomes a moment of trust between you and another human being. This is a privilege.

You don't just hear them, you listen to them, and actively listen to them. Be there for them and with them; one human to another.

That's what active listening is really all about.

Sure, there's the roadmap and the six basics; there's listening for details in nature, meanings in music, and empathy at the theatre; there's listening to difficult situations like criticism, intimacy, weaknesses, and future dreams from your love-partner and others; there's the reticular activating system, your focus and attention, the anterior cingulate gyrus, oxytocin and mirror neurons in your brain; and there's unconditional positive regard, listening for information, and listening for feelings; but it all boils down to this one thing.

Just be there.

Listen.

LISTENING QUOTES

There's a lot to take in and practice from this book. Here are some important listening quotes – from the take home messages – to read, think about and practice.

from CHAPTER ONE: Listening EARS

Listening is a gift we give to someone else.

Relationship listening is for sharing emotions, not for solving problems.

You can't control other people.

Listening is a one-way street. Traffic heads towards you.

Be comfortable with silence.

Shelve your judgments and beliefs to be a listening sponge.

Trust means keeping confidences. Always.

from CHAPTER TWO: Practicing Listening

Actively listen to open yourself to a whole world of beautiful moments.

The head and the heart work together in listening.

Every listening encounter is unique and special.

We naturally empathize with each other, if we let ourselves.

In listening, treat others the way you like to be treated.

from CHAPTER THREE: Listening to your Love-Partner

The love is in the listening and the trying.

Be gentle with each other.

Listening says I love you.

Keeping things bottled up comes at a cost.

If something difficult is being said, your job is to listen.

Listening can be an intimate act of love.

Listen to dreams and ideas. Soar together before considering reality.

from CHAPTER FOUR: The Science of Listening

When listening, only listen.

Empathy and compassion help us connect.

Eye contact is important; eyes are the mirror of the soul.

Beliefs and opinions make us different.

from CHAPTER FIVE: Deeper Listening

A person has feelings; don't walk away.

Listening is containing emotions for someone else.

Nobody wants to be alone.

Listening is shared vulnerability.

Listening preserves hope.

Just be there.

Notes and References

[1] Bentley, Sheila C. "Listening in the 21ˢᵗ Century." *International Journal of Listening* 14.1 (2000): 129-142.

[2] http://www.balancingaustralia.com.au/r-u-ok-day-2012/ retrieved 11 November 2017.

[3] Throughout this book, I use the words "emotions" and "feelings" interchangeably.

[4] See, for example, Loukopoulos, Loukia D., Key Dismukes, and Immanuel Barshi. *The multitasking myth: Handling complexity in real-world operations.* Ashgate Publishing, Ltd., 2009. And Crenshaw, Dave. *The myth of multitasking: How "doing it all" gets nothing done.* John Wiley & Sons, 2008.

[5] Caird, Jeff K., et al. "A meta-analysis of the effects of texting on driving." *Accident Analysis & Prevention* 71 (2014): 311-318.

[6] Cohen, Ronald A. "Neuropsychological Models of attention." *The neuropsychology of attention.* Springer US, 2014. 678-718 p697

[7] Charles Bell. Quoted in Sierhuis, Freya. *Passions and subjectivity in early modern culture.* Routledge, 2016. p5.

[8] Darwin, Charles *The expression of the emotions in man and animals.* Appleton & Co. New York 1897. p354

[9] Birdwhistell, Ray L. *Introduction to kinesics: An annotation system for analysis of body motion and gesture.* Department of State, Foreign Service Institute, 1952.

[10] This is supported by the scientific principles of neuroplasticity.

[11] See for example Neumann, Inga D. "Brain oxytocin mediates beneficial consequences of close social interactions: From maternal love and sex." *Hormones and social behaviour.* Springer Berlin Heidelberg,

(2008): 81-10, Gonzaga, Gian C., et al. "Romantic love and sexual desire in close relationships." *Emotion* 6.2 (2006): 163; and Carter, C. Sue. 163 "Neuroendocrine perspectives on social attachment and love." *Psychoneuroendocrinology* 23.8 (1998): 779-818. Also Savulescu, Julian, and Anders Sandberg. "Neuroenhancement of love and marriage: The chemicals between us." *Neuroethics* 1.1 (2008): 31-44. Nissen, Eva, et al. "Elevation of oxytocin levels early post-partum in women." *Acta obstetricia et gynecologica Scandinavica* 74.7 (1995): 530-533. Mikolajczak, Moïra, et al. "Oxytocin not only increases trust when money is at stake, but also when confidential information is in the balance." *Biological psychology* 85.1 (2010): 182-184 and Kosfeld, Michael, et al. "Oxytocin increases trust in humans." *Nature* 435.7042 (2005): 673-676.

[12] Williams, Caroline. "A user's guide to the mind." *New scientist* No 2989 4 October 2014, p37

[13] http://news.bbc.co.uk/1/hi/england/wear/4746665.stm. Retrieved September 22, 2017.

[14] https://www.livescience.com/29290-fatima-miracle.html Retrieved September 22, 2017.

[15] Rogers, Carl Ransom. *A theory of therapy, personality, and interpersonal relationships: As developed in the client-centered framework.* Vol. 3. New York: McGraw-Hill, 1959. p208.

[16] See Mikolajczak, Moïra, et al. "Oxytocin not only increases trust when money is at stake, but also when confidential information is in the balance." *Biological psychology* 85.1 (2010): 182-184 and Kosfeld, Michael, et al. "Oxytocin increases trust in humans." *Nature* 435.7042 (2005): 673-676.

[17] Plutchik, Robert. "The Nature of Emotions Human emotions have deep evolutionary roots, a fact that may explain their complexity and provide tools for clinical practice." *American scientist* 89.4 (2001): 344-350.

Printed in Australia
AUOW01n2226121217
292624AU00001B/1